BEING, MEANING,
AND BREATH

BEING, MEANING, AND BREATH

A Scientist Ponders the Harmony of Science and Faith

W. Scott Andrus

Mill City Press, Inc.
212 3rd Avenue North, Suite 290
Minneapolis, MN 55401
612.455.2294
www.millcitypublishing.com

ISBN-13: 978-1-937600-86-0
LCCN: 2012931977

Printed in the United States of America

For Marge, the love of my life

I am grateful for critical readings and discussions with The Reverend Thomas Woodward, Dr. Douglas Puryear, and Ms. Suzanne Marier (twice!) While they bear no responsibility for the book's shortcomings, they have contributed greatly to any coherence the reader may detect.

Mr. Juan Villalobos ably drew the figures.

CONTENTS

PREFACE

Theism: belief in the existence of a god or gods; specifically: belief in the existence of one God viewed as the creative source of man and the world who transcends yet is immanent in the world

Science: knowledge or a system of knowledge covering general truths or the operation of general laws esp. as obtained and tested through scientific method

Scientific method: principles and procedures for the systematic pursuit of knowledge involving the recognition and formulation of a problem, the collection of data through observation and experiment, and the formulation and testing of hypotheses [1]

I was a pretty docile Sunday school kid who grew up to be a scientist but remained a theist as defined above. Yes it is possible to be both: theism is not contradicted by the scientific method.

An atheist is the opposite of a theist. I have never felt the need to opt for atheism in response to anything I learned from science. But when I was eight or nine I did notice that there were some consistency issues. For example, I was taught in school that the earliest forms of life were microorganisms, which didn't seem to square with the biblical account of the Garden of Eden. But I didn't get too excited about this discrepancy; I thought maybe Adam and Eve were microorganisms. That may seem at first glance to be a clever hypothesis, particularly for a small child, but actually it won't work because microorganisms reproduce asexually. There are no male and female microorganisms. This has good and bad effects: no alimony battles, but also no love songs. If Adam and Eve had been microorganisms there would have been no need for Adam in Eve's Garden, and the story would have lost its flavor.

I went on to study physics and have always found it pretty easy to reconcile what I learned about science with the basics of religion as I learned them in mainline Protestant (Presbyterian and Lutheran in my

---

1   Merriam-Webster's Collegiate Dictionary,
© 1994 Merriam-Webster, Inc.

youth, later Episcopal) churches. The basics as I came to understand them did not include an insistence on the historical accuracy of the events recorded in Genesis; I realized quite early that the value of that record did not lie in telling us precisely how or when the universe was formed. It's more about why. I can also report this on the authority of a very prominent conservative religious figure (Chapter 9) who said almost exactly the same thing.

I thought most people understood this point. It's true that a jury in Dayton, Tennessee had convicted the schoolteacher John Scopes of teaching evolution and fined him a hundred dollars. There was a law in Tennessee against teaching anything that contradicted the account of Creation found in Genesis. But that was back in 1925, and even then the verdict was overturned on the face-saving ground that the fine was excessive.

Viewed with the perspective of its historical context the fine doesn't seem excessive at all. In a far worse judicial outrage, the ancient Greeks found Socrates guilty of corrupting the youth of Athens by teaching them the wrong things: in other words, of the same offense Scopes was later charged with. The cases were quite parallel: there was a theological component in Socrates's alleged offense, as in Scopes's. Socrates, like Scopes, wanted to go on teaching and would have been happy to get off with a fine. In fact he proposed this penalty – some friends had offered to put up the money – but the Athenians were much sterner than the Daytonians. Socrates was forced to put himself to death by drinking hemlock. By comparison, the Dayton court went easy on Scopes: his treatment would have been lenient even if he had paid his fine. Perhaps this is a sign of progress.

In 1967, the year I completed my doctorate in physics, Tennessee repealed the law against teaching evolution. By this time, I thought, general agreement – even if not unanimity – had evolved on the subject of evolution and more broadly on acceptance of scientific findings that appeared to contradict the fundamentalist understanding of the Bible. At the Lutheran college where I was an undergraduate, almost everyone, faculty and students, accepted evolution. Only two people walked out when a pro-evolution scene from the play "Inherit the Wind" was performed in the chapel. In my naivety I thought reason was prevailing.

The Resurgence of Intolerance

Today it is clear that I was too optimistic. There may have been general agreement at my college, but the 1925 outlook has made a comeback. A virulent strain of religious thinking that demands unquestioning belief in very dubious historical and moral precepts is becoming increasingly popular. A college in Virginia requires its students to sign a statement of faith including the proposition that Hell is a place where "all who die outside of Christ shall be confined in conscious torment for eternity."[2] Such a view imputes a remarkable degree of sadism to God in his treatment of most of his people: since Christianity is a minority religion worldwide, the majority are not only to be separated from God but tortured endlessly for their alleged theological misunderstanding. This is a hardnosed perspective, even harsher than that of the Athenians who condemned Socrates. Its adherents, not remotely satisfied that *they* believe what they believe, insist that *everyone* must believe as they do or suffer a fate far worse than death.

Intolerance is a common thread among many – though by no means all – religious people and is one of the gravest charges to be brought against religion. If the religious people in question are Christians, they probably view with contempt the efforts of Muslims to promote harsh sharia law. The contempt is likely to be mutual. Meanwhile, some in America today are active in trying to pass laws that are based on their narrow precepts and are binding on people of all persuasions.

Intolerance cuts both ways, of course. Opposing that of some religious zealots is a facile dismissal of *all* religious thinking. Each of these alternatives represents a sad and unnecessary sacrifice. However we were formed, we seem to have arrived at a state of advanced intelligence. Of course we have nothing much to compare our intelligence to, but we are able to use it to solve some interesting problems so it must in *some* sense be advanced. At least we're smarter than the other animals on this planet: show me a dolphin who can solve a partial differential equation. To waste this capacity, or to confine it within walls of narrow-minded bigotry, is a crime against whatever

---

2   Rosen, Hanna: "God and Country". *The New Yorker, June 27, 2005*

power placed us here and against ourselves. We have an obligation to use the minds we find ourselves equipped with.

This obligation doesn't justify the doctrinaire and unsupported dismissal of the spiritual realm. That's also wasteful: it discards millennia of profoundly thoughtful progress that has provided comfort, insight, guidance, and a better life to billions throughout the history of humanity. People who want to toss out the valuable perspective of religion generally claim that it is incompatible with things that we have come to know reliably from other sources. This reason would make sense if faith's boundaries were those understood by the majority in Dayton in 1925, or the faculty of Patrick Henry College in Virginia, but that's not the true envelope of religion, in 1925, today, or ever. It is not necessary to stray from traditional religion[3] in order to perceive the consistency and complementarity between rational thought and the religious understanding.

Core Beliefs

I plan to demonstrate this consistency and complementarity by examining core religious claims in the light of what we know – or think we know – from science. Let me make the goal clear. I'm not arguing that what we know from science *proves* religious statements. There's no proof; as discussed in the Afterword, we have no basis on which to be certain, one way or the other. But religion and science are meant to be harmonious, rather than discordant.

One difficulty in demonstrating this harmony needs to be dealt with right up front: different people regard different religious statements as core beliefs. It's not a new problem. Christianity was born in diversity and went on to schism. The early Christian churches struggled to reach agreement as to exactly what would be taught to their followers. In particular, there were subtleties around the relationship among the aspects of God that Christians contemplate: the Creator, the Christ, and the Holy Spirit – Father, Son, and Holy

---

3 Since I was reared in the Christian tradition, the religion discussed will be Christianity. Probably a similar development could be provided for other religions, but someone else would have to provide it.

Ghost, in the traditional formulation – because these three had to be unified somehow within the central idea of monotheism. These debates were intense and of course have not entirely subsided to this day. Judaism and Islam still criticize the Holy Trinity as a polytheistic concept. But a basic core body of doctrine was formulated and eventually summarized in the Nicene Creed.

The Nicene Creed has roots in the Creed of Nicaea, promulgated at the Council of Nicaea in the year 325 C.E.,[4] but in fact what we now call the Nicene Creed is an independent document, probably issued by the Council of Constantinople and made explicit by the Council of Chalcedon in 451 C.E. This Creed (more formally known as the Niceno-constantinopolitan Creed, a term that will not appear again in these pages) describes the one God in three persons. It is not a fringe document. It is accepted as authoritative by the Roman Catholic, Anglican, and major Protestant churches, and also to a considerable degree by the Eastern Orthodox. A modified clause asserting that the Holy Spirit proceeds "from the Father *and the son*" (*filioque*, in Latin) was added beginning in the sixth century and was the center of major controversy: some churches thought the Holy Spirit proceeds only from the Father. The entire difference was the insertion of the single word *filioque*. The *filioque* clause was given papal acceptance in the Eleventh Century and is now accepted fully by all Western churches, while the Eastern churches accept it with conditions. Apart from this very technical exception the Nicene Creed is not controversial within Christianity: pretty much everyone accepts it. It is not novel or revisionist. It can be said to define the core beliefs of the Christian mainstream. So we'll choose to base our discussion on this document.

The Nicene Creed summarizes the essence of the great religious revelations of the Bible as traditionally understood by Christian churches. Certainly no kind of scientific analysis can prove it, but we will see that the statements it makes fit quite comfortably into a rational worldview. Despite its tradition and orthodoxy, nothing known to science today can either refute it or establish it. This fact is not universally obvious, in part because the language and symbolism are ancient. Much of the Creed's language is

---

4   We'll use B.C.E. (for Before Current Era) and C.E. (for Current Era) in place of B.C. and A.D., respectively.

metaphorical, so it is subject to a different level of verification from that addressed by science. I will discuss elements of the Creed in terms of the physical world as we are coming to understand it today on the basis of the scientific method. We'll see that this process is quite straightforward and can be accomplished without rejecting any part of the Creed or any well-supported scientific conclusion.

In carrying out this program we do have to recognize what scripture represents. People regard scripture as inspired by God, but they understand inspiration in different ways. Some believe that the inspired word of God cannot possibly contain a word that is not literally true. That's not my understanding. Scripture is not a stenographic record of God's utterances, but the best thinking of the times when its inspired authors set it down. They were inspired to think and to write; they were not told precisely *what* to think or write. As a result, the authors of the various books of the Bible were limited to what was known in their times about the physical world.

Those times range from just over three thousand years ago to shortly after the lifetime of Jesus. There is evidence of human spiritual stirrings dating back 35,000 years, and without question the understandings described in the Bible owe an enormous debt to questions and tentative answers during those earlier millennia. What Christians depend on was set down in a brief spasm of writing – the Bible includes nothing written in the last nineteen hundred years – but its insights have formed gradually over a much longer time. These insights have universal relevance, but we cannot expect them to incorporate everything we've learned in the last two millennia.

In what follows we'll take the Nicene Creed as a summary of core beliefs. We'll attempt to suggest the larger envelope of Christianity by examining statements about God in the light of today's scientific knowledge. We'll talk about God in the three roles the Creed envisions: as creator, redeemer, and spiritual counselor. Since the language of the Nicene Creed and its scriptural underpinnings is many centuries old, we'll reexamine some of these statements in modern language. Taking the Creed as a summary of core beliefs and at the same time respecting the results of scientific inquiry, we'll discover that the Creed's statements do not conflict with anything that is known today on a rational basis. Not only is there no inconsistency, but in fact the two approaches complement each other in producing a broader understanding.

I should make it clear that I didn't write this book solely as a scientist, but also as a human. Science has been my discipline for half a dozen decades. It conditions the way I think about things, including things that are not explicitly matters of science. And so you will find that for pages at a time, I discuss various issues without mentioning energy, or matter, or any of the things science typically talks about. My viewpoint is still that of a scientist, even when I'm discussing things about which science is silent.

[A note on etiquette: In attempting to support these views I have not hesitated to draw on insights from any source I found useful. At the same time this is a personal perspective, not a scholarly review. I have come to the views described here over a period of several decades, and I cannot always trace the sources. Where I can do so I have cited them – of course with the understanding that they are not accountable for my errors or for my views. But the views are mine, whether or not they are original. Accordingly, I have not bothered to use tentative language. I have stated declaratively things that may be controversial. Naturally I recognize that I'm not necessarily right about any of this, and I'm not focusing on staying in total accord with the dogma of any church. But since everything here represents my thinking, in the interest of neatness I have not cluttered the manuscript by preceding each statement by the words, "I think…"]

INTRODUCTION

Six thousand and fourteen years, nine months, and twenty-six days ago[5] God said, "Let there be light." The universe immediately came into being. Within six days Earth was populated by plants, animals, fish, birds, creepy-crawlies, and one each of men, women, and talking snakes. Each creature was individually hand-crafted at the moment of its creation to be in perfect harmony with the environment in which it found itself, so no change in the characteristics of any species was ever needed. In the next four thousand years reason and natural law were regularly flouted, God had folksy conversations with favored individuals, and clear evidence that things had not happened as reported was planted by a deity who seemed eager to confuse us. This deity dictated to stenographers one book whose contents are to be taken as literal, infallible, and good for all time – every single word. The book is a perfect finished product. No additions, changes, or strange interpretations may be tolerated. It's inadvisable to think too much, and science should be viewed with particular suspicion if not hostility. There are questions that should not be asked and people – such as those who ask questions – with whom it is dangerous to associate. My church's customs reflect the laws of God; any deviation is evidence of evil influence or perhaps outright demonic possession.

That is a description, exaggerated only very slightly if at all, of the philosophical basis of some people's lives. We could call it the neoTennessee approach to religion. It takes literally the account of a six-day creation and all that goes with it, and features a narrow-minded suspicion of more critically considered interpretation. It assumes that God himself dictated the Pentateuch – the books of Genesis, Exodus, Leviticus, Numbers, and Deuteronomy – and that what they contain is literal and infallible.

---

5   I recorded this sentence August 17, 2011, on the authority of the Bible-based timetable presented by Bishop James Ussher.

Modern biblical scholarship, on the other hand, suggests that the first five books of the Bible are a synthesis of works by at least four authors, writing in different centuries. These authors – their identities are unknown – are denoted in in one schema as J for Jahwist; E for Elohist; P for Priestly; and D for Deuteronomist. J is responsible for much of Genesis. Writing in elegant style, J calls God by the name Yahweh (formerly rendered Jehovah) and writes from the viewpoint of the southern Hebrew kingdom, Judah. E initially refers to God as Elohim and writes from the viewpoint of the northern kingdom. J and E show a human-like God and contain similar events with variant details. P focuses on genealogies and lists and describes a distant and demanding God. Most of the law in Leviticus is attributed to P. D contains the book of Deuteronomy as well as biblical books outside the Pentateuch. The details of the schema are still debated and don't concern us here, but most modern scholars agree that the Pentateuch has multiple human authors supporting various points of view.

Ignorant Armies

The idea of multiple authorship is anathema to people who insist on a literal and infallible Bible. For a while, the number of people with literalist perspectives decreased as a result of better education and freer opportunities to express dissenting views. But today their numbers seem to be back on the rise, in part because of the ability of well-heeled propagandists to reach a mass audience. As a result we have come to the point where many people imagine that the kind of statement that began this introduction actually defines western religion.

An alternative view is fed by rebellion against the dogmatism of the first. (Since extremism breeds reaction, the rebels are often the rebellious children of dogmatists of the first type.) The alternative view is characterized by equally ill-founded dogmatism:

All *religion is primitive superstition. Scientific method tells us that the universe is a pointless cosmic burp. There is no room merely to be skeptical or doubtful about spiritual twaddle. Rather, the idea of God can be dismissed a priori as absurd, as incompatible with what we know. Advances in cosmology,* *geology, biology, chemistry, and physics have removed the mystery from questions of how the universe works and how we got here. The universe came into being on its own with no cause, no purpose, no intent, no meaning, and no goal. Morality is whatever it takes to survive. With the mystery and magic taken away, God no longer has a function:* "Je n'ai pas besoin de cette hypothese."[6]

If we look only at these polar opposite world views, it seems that theism and rationality, religion and science, cannot be reconciled and that we have to choose one and reject the other. A lot of people who accept scientific results but do not understand them imagine that spiritual thinking is demonstrably false to fact, that science proves religion to be nonsense. And a lot of people who accept religion imagine that scientific results are the snares of Satan. Instead of a search for truth by all available means we have ignorant armies, clashing by night.

The Mind and the Spirit

For a long time the religious army had the preponderance of physical power, and it regularly met rational criticism with beheadings, torture, burning, vilification, and exclusion from society. Even today, even in America where separation of church and state is supposed to be set in constitutional granite, governments take actions under cover of alleged religious truth. These actions can range from something as harmless as supporting a Christmas crèche to such major abuses as denial of marriage rights to an unconventional minority. Until very recently people could go to prison, where they were quite likely to be assaulted if not killed, for private behavior officially deemed contrary to God's will. Since some time in the Middle Ages it has been a high stakes power struggle and in many places it still is. The religious party has rarely hesitated to exercise its figurative nuclear option by condemning its opponents to eternal hellfire – or at least "conscious torment for eternity." Acceptance of religion is associated with certain burdens,

---

6 When Napoleon remarked to Pierre-Simon Laplace (1749-1827), "You have written this huge book on the system of the world without once mentioning the author of the universe," Laplace famously replied, "I have no need for that hypothesis." This statement has become an atheists' rallying cry.

and one of the heaviest is association with some of the self-described religious people. And some in the rationalist party, inventors of the *real* nuclear option, are fully as obnoxious.

This suggests that we're all in a bind. The character Levin, in Leo Tolstoy's *Anna Karenina*, searches his soul this way:

Ever since, by his beloved brother's deathbed, Levin had first glanced into these questions of life and death…he had been stricken with horror, not so much of death, as of life, without any knowledge of whence, and why, and how, and what it was. The physical organization, its decay, the indestructibility of matter, the law of the conservation of energy, evolution, were the words which usurped the place of his old belief. These words and the ideas were very well for intellectual purposes. But for life they yielded nothing, and Levin felt suddenly like a man who has exchanged his warm fur cloak for a muslin garment…Levin had never lost his sense of terror at his lack of knowledge.

It is natural to want to believe in a loving Creator, to want to believe that our existence is informed by some semblance of meaning. But the things we learn by the methods of science are compelling. There is a strong sense that science is telling us the truth and that it would be absurd to turn our backs on these truths. Which must be given up, the mind or the spirit?

Neither. The bind is apparent, not real. In considerable measure it results from the fact that our religious teachings are old and are traditionally expressed in ancient ways. The language of science is today's language. A synthesis of the two therefore requires reexamination of the old truths of religion, so they can be phrased in a way that allows us to see their consistency with the latest insights from science. It doesn't have to be a problem. Despite all the adversarial posturing, it is not difficult to be both a theist and a scientist. We can accept the rational approach without rejecting the spiritual insights of religion. Rationality is a way of arriving at, or at least seeking, truth. Religion is another, among other things.[7] Rationality is about demonstrable facts and the relationships

---

7 Religion goes beyond truth-seeking and also offers suggestions as to our response to the truths uncovered. Science as science does not offer suggestions, though many scientists, being humans, do take this step.

between them. The objects of religion are not as sharply focused but are by no means unimportant. The rational and the spiritual are complementary.

This is not to say that spiritual precepts can be proved scientifically. They cannot, any more than scientific statements can look to religion for support. But neither are core religious concepts refuted by what we know from science. Their language is metaphorical, making scientific verification pretty much a non-starter. Still, scientific methods and results can shed considerable light on what theists believe. Nobody has to abandon the spiritual in order to think rationally, or vice versa. The mind and the spirit are not hats we wear on alternate occasions. You don't have to check your brains at the church door on the way in; we all need to refuse to accept nonsense. And you don't have to check your humanity at the door on the way out; churches are useless if they don't prepare us to act decently all week.

The rejection, in the name of religion, of God's great gift of human intelligence is *not* in fact the traditional pattern. The earliest thinkers, thousands of years ago, used everything they could find at a time when there wasn't much available. We will describe a somewhat more recent example of intelligence in the service of the spiritual. It is only in the past millennium, more or less, that some have come to see theism as irrational, rationality as atheistic, and the two as incompatible and mutually hostile. Now that there is so much more information, it seems that the competitive instincts on both sides have been aroused.

Definitions of Truth

If theism really were irrational – that is, contrary to reason – then it could be held only by beings who rejected their own power to reason. Such people exist, as we shall see, but they must not be allowed to define theism. And if theism were *purely* rational it would offer nothing not already available from science. That's not the case either. I intend to demonstrate that we can choose both theism and rationality. For that purpose it will be useful to explain a bit about the scientific approach, which will play a major role in the rest of the book. So in this introduction I will sketch the methods scientists use to gain their insights, and compare these insights to spiritual insights obtained by a different route.

Religion and science ask and answer different questions, use different techniques, and have different standards of truth. They respond to different issues. Their most fundamental answers do not conflict. Religion is ultimately concerned with the most crucial philosophical questions: "Why are we here?" "What is expected of us?" "How are we to act – what is the good life?" "To whom do we answer?" The fact that science offers no direct help with these questions should not lead anyone to believe that the questions are meaningless or trivial.

Science is interested in another sort of question: "How do physical causes produce physical effects?" "What actually happened in the first instants of the universe's existence?" "What, exactly, is happening beneath what is apparent to the eye, and how has the present physical state of affairs gotten to look the way it does?" These are also important and nontrivial questions. Religion has little useful to say about them. Genesis was written for a totally different purpose. It speaks in metaphor, providing enlightenment rather than scientific fact.

Science's definition of truth is radically different from religion's. There is widespread misunderstanding about the nature of science. Many think that science deals with proven certainties and that scientific measurements are exact. In fact, though, any measurement in science comes with stated limits of error: a quantity is said to have a certain value plus or minus a certain percentage. And that certain percentage is never zero; no measurement is perfectly exact. As to proven certainties: nothing is ever proven in science. Truth is a matter of successive approximation. A hypothesis is proposed tentatively for consideration on the basis that it seems potentially useful. Its logical sense and consistency with available observational data are studied. If it has not been refuted by this time – most hypotheses are – it may eventually begin to gain some acceptance, particularly if it is capable of predicting the results of additional observations suggested by the hypothesis. Its acceptance will grow if observation or experiment continues to support it. But it is always at risk: experiment can at any time force changes in the concept.

Spiritual answers are not at risk in the same way, because they are not susceptible to this kind of experimental verification or refutation. Science asks tight, focused questions, even when it is contemplating enormous issues like the universe as a whole. Spiritual questions are more open-ended, less limited, harder to define. Experience is helpful, but scientific observation can do no more than shine a little light around the edges of the spiritual. Truth has a different meaning. We ask whether the answers hold together in some kind of consistent pattern. There can be – must be – mystery, but there should not be frank illogic. And we ask whether a life built on religious answers is in some sense a better life than one built on an alternative: greed, hedonism, ego, dialectical materialism, golf… These are not questions that are usefully addressed by science, but on the other hand religion cannot tell us how cells become malignant and thus how cancer might be cured. Perhaps faith healing can contribute to a patient's recovery, but it is no substitute for the scientific advances of modern medicine. Spiritual truths have to do with experience, inner feelings, our response to revelation.

As the questions of religion are not usefully addressed by science, so the questions of science are not well addressed by religion. When science tells us that the universe is fourteen billion years old the appropriate responses are: "How do you know?" "How good are the data, and the analyses, on which this number is based?" "How precise is this determination: could it be fifteen billion years, or thirteen billion? Can we say it's fourteen and a half billion rather than fourteen billion?" Religion is, or should be, silent on such matters.

For the record, the currently favored number for the age of the universe is 13.73 ± 0.12 billion years. This represents a precision of about 0.9%. Rounding to the nearest billion, I will generally abbreviate this as fourteen billion years from now on. What's two hundred and seventy million years among friends?

One Reality, Two Narratives

We have on the one hand the scriptural account of a few days' events leading to modern conditions after six thousand years. Confronting this is a description from science, incomplete but compelling, of billions of years of successive processes leading to the same conditions. Can these two narratives be talking about the same reality?

Sure they can. Remember the story of the blind men encountering an elephant. Depending on which part of the elephant each man feels he decides that an elephant is a wall, or a tree trunk, or a rope, or a spear. They're all correct as far as they go and the full story of the elephant contains these elements: body, leg, tail, tusk, respectively.

In our case the scriptural narrative is telling the story of a benevolent creator motivated by love to make a home for his creatures. The time element is inconsequential and the archaic physical concepts are not central to the narrative. The home is systematically assembled and then the creatures, finally including humankind, are established in it. The scientific narrative has a totally different perspective, describes a different part of the elephant. The focus is on the physical processes, how long they took, what forces were in play. Motivation does not enter the picture. I don't mean that science shows that there is no motivation; I mean that the motivation, if there was one, is outside the range of the techniques of science. The scientific narrative is all about the physics at first, and then the chemistry, the biology, the psychology, the sociology. We'll say a bit about each of these as we sketch the story. Remember that while the narratives appear very different they are describing aspects of the same elephant. They are both true.

Despite the difference in approach there is synergy between the spiritual answers and those of science. Science can tell us that the universe has been evolving for fourteen billion years and that humankind is a phenomenon of the last thousandth of one percent of that time. Religion can neither support nor refute that statement, but can help us to see ourselves as the culmination of a plan that pointed to us over all those eons, and that suggests a response in our lives. It is no more reasonable for religious devotees to try to tell us that the fourteen billion years was really only six thousand, in the face of clear evidence to the contrary, than it is for scientific devotees to tell us that there is no content in questions about the meaning of life or the responsibilities of humans. The meaning of life is outside the scope of science but is not outside the scope of human consideration.

The spiritual approach must not reject information that is solidly based in rationality. The theological insights of humans can evolve, even though we understand God to be eternal and unchanging, because humankind is neither. We have no reason to be afraid of theological evolution. The changing questions and answers of faith reflect progress in human understanding. Different ways of thinking about God, ways the religious thinkers of past millennia could not know, are available to us now. No human understanding will ever be final: God is beyond not only our current understanding but even our potential comprehension. But that doesn't mean we should limit our range to human concepts and images that were frozen two thousand years ago. Everything that is true in the religious sphere must be consistent with everything that is true in any other sphere. Truth is truth.

If we learn from well-settled scientific consensus that the universe is billions of years old, we must reconcile our religious beliefs with that fact. We will find that this reconciliation does not require us to abandon anything essential to our faith, any core belief. Why should it matter to our faith that the universe is old? But the reconciliation certainly does require us to abandon the traditional insistence that the Bible is a literal historical record, dictated word by word to passive scribes by an omniscient deity. The Bible contains some material that seems to be historically accurate, but its historical narrative as a whole cannot be relied on and is not essential to our core beliefs.

The Method of Science

Not that any statement of science is guaranteed to be correct. It's important to understand how scientific progress is made. Begin with this: strictly speaking there is ultimately no such thing as a scientific fact. Despite what some people think, scientific statements are always tentative. Every scientist knows that what was discovered yesterday may need to be modified tomorrow to bring it closer to the truth. The final picture is continually approached but never fully reached. Ultimate truth recedes as we pursue it.

This is a process that advances in steps, and sometimes the advance requires us to take one step back to achieve two steps forward. But even then we do not encounter situations where an entire branch of knowledge based on solid observational evidence is thrown away. Instead of discarding former insights when correction is needed, we apply new observations and analyses, refining and extending yesterday's understanding to produce tomorrow's. As we narrow down our observations we may find that the universe is fifteen billion years old, or thirteen billion. But it will not turn out to be six thousand years old; that would be inconsistent with too many other things we know from observation. The conclusions of science are not rendered worthless even though every statement is subject to improvement.

Yet the unnecessary struggle between spiritual and scientific approaches continues. As I write, science textbooks are being defaced, by government fiat, with labels stating that evolution is "merely" a theory. That view, expressing warfare between science and religion, is correct only in the narrowest sense. While some of the detailed elements of evolution as it is currently understood may need modification, the concept itself is based on a vast number of careful observations and is on very firm ground. Evolution *is* a theory, but this statement misleads by implying that a theory is no more than some scientist's dyspeptic fantasy. The word "theory," which is used loosely and inaccurately to refer to all sorts of speculations, in fact has a precise definition. Scientists have to speculate – that's how new ideas come into being – but in science a theory is a far different animal from a speculation.

A scientific theory is a statement supported by observational evidence and logical (usually mathematical) reasoning and capable of making predictions about the results of observations to be performed in the future. Often these observations are based on laboratory experiments, but sometimes all we can do is look at natural phenomena: supernovae, fossils, geologic formations, ancient artifacts... In either case, the theory launches itself from the observation to tell us what will be observed in situations that have not yet been studied. If theory predicts something that doesn't pan out – that differs from the result of a subsequent observation – then the theory has been refuted. A speculation can lead easily to a hypothesis but a hypothesis does not attain the status of a theory until it has been tested over a period of time and has withstood critical scrutiny, typically from rival scientists who are eager to show that it is wrong. Scientists are competitive folks, and the Church is not the only institution with devil's advocates.

If it passes all its logical and observational tests, a hypothesis is eventually conceded to be consistent with everything that is known *so far*, and can be talked about as a theory. But it can never be considered final, even though a thousand experiments may confirm it. In science nothing is ever finally proved; nothing is a fact in the sense that it cannot be challenged by new evidence. (The basic concept of evolution comes as close to this status as anything I can think of.) As soon as *one* new observation shows a result inconsistent with the implications of the theory, it is the theory that is overdue for modification. Thus, while it can never be proved, the theory can be *dis*proved by a single observational counterexample. That doesn't mean the theory is worthless, and it is typically not radically abandoned, because it has already been shown to have value. Rather, ways are sought to modify the theory, keeping what works and finding a new approach to solve the inconsistency that has been found. The evidence with which the theory is consistent is combined with the results of the new experiment to develop an extended theory consistent with all evidence available. This is not necessarily a simple process. It often takes decades, sometimes centuries, to develop the new theory. And when the new theory is finally found, it is no more final than its predecessor. Rather, more experiments are performed, until a new inconsistency is found, and the process is repeated indefinitely.

Real Theories

Here's an example of the method: Newton's Theory of Universal Gravitation, which had stood for four centuries, was replaced by Einstein's General Theory of Relativity when subtle observations showed the need for a modification. Einstein's theory, now less than one century old, will no doubt need further refinement; it is showing signs of strain when applied to events in the first fractions of a second of the universe's existence. That is enough to indicate that a better theory is needed, even though general relativity has been confirmed by many observations and works very well after time's first microsecond. Newton's theory wasn't wrong: in the domain where it could be applied in Newton's time it passed every test and shed great light on the universe. We still use it in most situations because it gives the same results as Einstein's theory and is easier to apply. Where they give different results, we use general relativity. Einstein's theory isn't wrong either, though it will need to be extended. That won't be an easy job, and perhaps it will take centuries to get it right, but the extension is necessary.

Similarly, the Theory of Evolution has been refined and extended many times. Scientists are actively engaged in this task. The bare fact that the process of evolution takes place is difficult to dispute. It is denied primarily by people who fear the implication, well supported by evidence, that mankind may have arisen from lower animals. This concern is hard to understand. Why should it be troubling that God produced us in steps from earlier life forms? But many people do find it troubling, because it's different from what they were taught. The denial of evolution, then, is based on bias, not evidence. Absent this concern, I doubt that many would deny the process of evolution.

But filling in the details of the process is an endless task. We understand evolution today to a depth that was unavailable to Darwin. We also understand that, with all its extensions, what we know about evolution does not yet give a complete description of everything that happens. There are still questions with no agreed answers, such as when and how often distinct species arise. But there are always open questions in science; that is the nature of the beast.

The Theory of Evolution will not disappear, even though refinements of detail are constantly being debated. Though nothing in science is a proven fact, the general outline of a theory as well-supported as evolution can be taken as factual for all practical purposes. Every scientific theory is an approximation, subject to the eventual need for further refinement in a process that does not end. The truth doesn't change; we just gain a more complete picture of it. While the findings of any human endeavor are tentative, we cannot expect well-founded scientific truths to be discarded root and branch. And just as our scientific understanding must always grow to remain consistent with all reliable observations, our understanding of God's workings must always grow to remain consistent with everything we have learned from any reliable source. God doesn't change; we hope to gain a somewhat more complete picture of his workings.

Pseudotheories

In contrast to the rigorously vetted scientific system that text book labels dismiss as "mere theory," two pseudoscientific systems are being promoted on what are really theological grounds, with no true scientific basis. We can call them pseudotheories because neither meets the definition of a theory. They share certain similarities as well as some differences.

The first pseudoscientific system, intelligent design, is primarily a statement about so-called guided evolution. The foundation notion in this case is that the universe develops generally as described by conventional science but that God intervenes at every moment to steer events toward the result he plans. In the case of guided evolution, this means accepting the fact that evolution occurred and produced mankind while insisting that such a thing could never have come about on its own: God had to "guide" it to bring about the situation we now observe.

It's no great stretch for theists to accept that the Creator may have guided the development of his creation. I don't know any way to prove he didn't. The problem comes when some of its adherents go on to assert that there is solid scientific evidence for intelligent design. They point to a complex structure or process in living organisms – examples range from the mammalian eye, to the flagella that allow a bacterium to move, to the amazing sequence of chemical events that coagulate the blood and limit bleeding from a wound – and claim that it could not possibly have evolved without the intelligent intervention of a higher power. That sounds like a "proof" of God's activity, but many advocates of intelligent design avoid the question of God, perhaps because they prefer to fight one battle at a time. Finding it politic not to claim that intelligent design provides objective support for theism, they deny that the intelligent higher power is necessarily God. One can speculate on what the power would then be. Curiously, one suggestion is that aliens from space somehow seeded Earth with living material. That of course merely reduces the question to one of what still higher power designed the space aliens…

Virtually everyone in the scientific community finds the arguments for the scientific necessity of intelligent design unconvincing. Mechanisms have been suggested for evolution of an eye, for example, without divine guidance. In any case, you can't really support a hypothesis simply by claiming that there is no other possible explanation for what is observed. Lack of complete understanding is no excuse for abandoning the methods of science. There is no way to demonstrate by observation that no alternative explanation exists. Moreover, the concept of intelligent design could never be considered a scientific theory, because it is incapable of predicting the results of experiments to be performed or observations to be made. Intelligent design should not even be characterized as a hypothesis. The role of a scientific hypothesis is to become a theory when enough evidence is accumulated, so a hypothesis must be a candidate theory, capable of being supported or refuted by evidence. If it's not at risk of being refuted it's not a theory or even a hypothesis. The notion that intelligent design, which cannot be supported or refuted by evidence, should be considered a scientific advance beyond the Theory of Evolution is nonsense. It is equally absurd to characterize intelligent design as a competitor, or an alternative, to the Theory of Evolution.

Intelligent design does not contradict any scientific observation, nor is there scientific support for it. It merely places God, or someone, at the controls, rather than allowing the universe to respond solely to mindless forces. Let us be clear: it is not a necessary tenet of the Theory of Evolution that evolution always proceeds randomly and without guidance. There is no evidence for – or against – that claim. The theory shows the process by which species, including our own, evolved from earlier, more primitive, forms of life. The evidence that this process occurred is overwhelming.

Cardinal Christoph Schonborn has recently stated, in an Op-Ed piece in the New York Times, that an insistence on random coincidence as the basis of our development is incompatible with Roman Catholic doctrine. This would not rule out evolution; basically he was supporting guided evolution and he did not claim that there is scientific proof of this concept. As far as science is concerned an intelligent designer may or may not be influencing the development of the universe. Science can never decide this matter. As a theist, I think there may be some truth in intelligent design, to the extent that God may will a particular universe to evolve. But this is a religious view, not based on any scientific evidence. No precept of science insists that science is the *only* way of knowing truth, though that may be the poorly founded opinion of some scientists. A scientist, or anyone else, who claims that evolution has expelled God from the universe goes far beyond any statement he can support with evidence.

It is precisely the fact that it cannot be subjected to scientific verification that makes teaching of intelligent design inappropriate in a science class. Intelligent design may be regarded as philosophical, theological, or religious, but since it is untestable by the methods of science it cannot be regarded as scientific. A cardinal may require his flock to believe in intelligent design, but that's a matter of institutional religious discipline. Whatever degree of truth it may contain, intelligent design cannot be tested by the methods of science, so it has nothing to do with the teaching of science.

Another problem is that some have used intelligent design as a smokescreen to cover the surreptitious introduction into scientific discussion and teaching of something even more egregious.

The second, older, and more egregious pseudoscientific system being promoted is "creation science,"[8] which dismisses the findings of real science and insists that Genesis, and indeed the Old Testament in its entirety, must be read as a literal and historical description of how and when the world and its contents assumed their present physical form. The creation of heaven and earth in a few days; the instantaneous

---

8   I am unable to record this misuse of the term "science" without quotation marks.

appearance of Adam and of Eve from one of his ribs; the continuous chronology that permits creation to be assigned a precise date only a few millennia ago: all are tenets of "creation science."

There is no serious observational or experimental evidence for this view. It is based on the principle that any passage in the Bible, read in the most literal way, overrides the evidence arising from all the observation and experiment that could ever be performed. Indeed we are surrounded by convincing observational evidence – we'll discuss a bit of geological evidence later – that the claims of "creation science" are unsupportable. "Creation science" rejects all the evidence. It is anyone's privilege to reject the use of observation, but to do this is to reject science itself and to reject it radically. There is no such thing as science that rejects observation. The term "science" should not be used to characterize the *rejection* of science. To teach this usage in a science classroom is, to put it mildly, inappropriate.

Proponents of "creation science" and intelligent design insist that science classes should "teach the controversy." The suggestion that all sides in a controversy should be taught is seductive but in this case misapplied. The Theory of Evolution, as propounded by Darwin and continuously developed to the present day, has many scientific controversies within it, but none of them involves intelligent design. Scientists argue about important details such as exactly how new species appear, how stable species are, how often new ones arise. But there is no controversy in science as to whether evolution occurs; this is obvious to everyone who takes a serious and unbiased look at the evidence. "Creation science" cannot reasonably be taught in a science class as an alternative to evolution because "creation science" is the radical rejection of science.

Intelligent design cannot properly be taught in a science class because it has no basis in science and cannot, even in principle, be scientifically tested. Teaching of intelligent design reduces to the making of statements about the activities of God. It may make sense to teach it in religious instruction, but certainly never in a science class. Since "creation science" is definitively ruled out by the facts we know, there is no excuse for teaching it anywhere except as a discredited notion of possible historical interest.

STRUCTURAL BASIS:
The Nicene Creed

The text of the Nicene Creed is:

We believe in one God, the Father, the Almighty, maker of heaven and earth, of all that is, seen and unseen.

We believe in one Lord, Jesus Christ, the only Son of God, eternally begotten of the Father, God from God, Light from Light, true God from true God, begotten, not made, of one Being with the Father. Through him all things were made. For us and for our salvation he came down from heaven: by the power of the Holy Spirit he became incarnate from the Virgin Mary, and was made man. For our sake he was crucified under Pontius Pilate; he suffered death and was buried. On the third day he rose again in accordance with the Scriptures; he ascended into heaven and is seated at the right hand of the Father. He will come again in glory to judge the living and the dead, and his kingdom will have no end.

We believe in the Holy Spirit, the Lord, the giver of life, who proceeds from the Father and the Son. With the Father and the Son he is worshipped and glorified. He has spoken through the Prophets. We believe in one holy catholic and apostolic Church. We acknowledge one baptism for the forgiveness of sins. We look for the resurrection of the dead, and the life of the world to come. Amen

I hope it's clear that I'm not claiming science and religion have nothing to say to one another. They have a great deal to say to one another. Accordingly, I will confront statements of the Nicene Creed with scientists' understanding of similar issues. That confrontation is the structural basis of this book. Right now I'll just sketch the outline. The discussion will play out in more detail in what follows.

To begin with, a small example of faulty dialog between science and religion. When I was in college, a history professor told us that medieval milking stools had three legs solely because people wanted to commemorate the Holy Trinity. As a physics major, I tried to explain to him that a three-legged stool is ideally adapted for stable function in a place, like a dairy barn, which (in medieval times) had a rough unlevel floor. A four-legged stool, like a modern restaurant table, will rock unless the legs have accurate lengths and the floor is flat. A two-legged stool can't stand on its own. But a three-legged stool stands without wobbling on any reasonably horizontal surface, even if its legs are of differing lengths. That's what you need when milking a cow: stability that you don't have to think about, so you can concentrate on not spilling the milk or getting hoof prints on your body.

Medieval people were no doubt eager to commemorate the Holy Trinity, but they did this while using stools that would be stable in use. They had milking to get done – any dairy farmer will tell you that cows *must* be milked on schedule – and this was as much a part of their lives as their religious devotion. My history professor was never convinced. As far as he was concerned milking stools pointed to an obsession with the Holy Trinity, not a practical engineering sense.[9] In his mind, apparently, it couldn't be both.

But it *can* be both. As we consider core elements of traditional theism in the light of current knowledge, we will find no contradiction between theism and any result of science or rationality. Actually, it seems to me that as one learns more one sees these approaches converging toward a consistent world view. Milking stools exhibit stability *and* commemorate the Holy Trinity. At the very least, it's clear that no inconsistency arises. Theism is never proved – no attempt should be made to prove it – but it is certainly never *dis*proved.

We will look at how scientific thought can lead to a broadened perspective, one that can enhance our understanding of some of the things asserted by the Nicene Creed. This short statement of the elements of Christian faith is organized in terms of the three persons of the Holy

---

9 One could even speculate that the professor had things backward. The number three was prominent in people's minds before the beginning of the Christian era, at least partly because of the properties of triangles, which give three-legged stools their stability. Perhaps the stability of milking stools contributed to the concept of the Trinity. If a four-legged stool were the most stable, might the triune God have become a tetragonal God?

Trinity: God the Father, God the Son, and God the Holy Spirit, who are understood to make up a single God in three persons. The idea of three persons has been troubling over the centuries to some, including Jews and Muslims, because it can be understood – Christians would say *mis*understood – to represent a polytheistic group: three gods.

The concept of the *persona*, a term coined by Carl Jung, is helpful here. A *persona* was the mask worn by an Etruscan mime: the stylized comedy and tragedy masks you see today in poster designs for theatrical productions. The individual behind the masks was the same actor seen in different roles. Christians relate to the one god variously in each of his three *personae*, or persons. The personae make God more tangible, more approachable. We have experience relating to a father, or a son, or perhaps even a spirit. We can see a progression from *persona* to *persona* – from creation to redemption to guidance – in the text of the Nicene Creed. This book will follow the same progression with a section corresponding to each paragraph of the Creed.

The Persons of the Creed

The Creed's first paragraph states simply that God is the creator of all that is. Scripture is less terse, generously providing in Genesis not just one but two accounts of creation. The accounts conflict because they were written at different times, by different authors, with different metaphorical intent. The bottom line is that the world we live in is a gift from a loving creator. But here we discuss the saga of creation as it is now understood on the basis of scientific advances, focusing on facts rather than metaphor. We note that every material thing in the universe, including even those exhibiting life itself, obeys ordinary physical laws. There is no miracle in the sense of the discarding of normal physics.

The meaning of the gift is mysterious until in the second paragraph of the Creed we come to understand that the meaning of being became incarnate in a human. The narrative of Jesus's words and actions, culminating in his offering of himself as a martyr and his subsequent resurrection in and for his followers, reveals the hope of humanity.

The Creed's final paragraph describes the presence of the Holy Spirit and the human response. Recognizing that the Spirit is the day-to-day connection between humans and God, we seek a fuller appreciation of the overall scriptural revelation and the path we are called to take. At the same time we will see a progression from creation of the physical universe, to the appearance of life, and finally to the emergence of humanity and of culture in the last brief fraction of the total saga.

We will take a section of this book to expand on each paragraph of the Creed. Section 1, "The Ground of Being," concentrates on the Father; Section 2, "The Meaning of Being," on the Son; Section 3, "The Breath of Being," on the Holy Spirit. Here is a brief taste of what is to come in those sections.

The Father. The Creed sees God the Father as the creator of the universe and "all that is, seen and unseen," and thus as the father of all. This symbol was conceived at a time when fatherhood was seen as the ultimate in creativity. In earlier times motherhood received its due measure of respect. But in the first millennium B.C.E. and the first century C.E., when the books that eventually became the Bible were written, people spoke and acted as if the father had more of a creative role in the birth of a child than the mother. This amusing notion survives in symbolic descriptions of God as a father. Even today a priest who speaks of God as "the father *and mother* of us all" can expect criticism from some parishioners and colleagues. The creative progenitor, the loving guide, the feudal lord, occasionally the demanding master: all these and more are implied in the concept of God the father. It is a powerful and compelling symbol.

And of course it is a symbol. God bears even less resemblance to the white-bearded old man of tradition than Jesus of Nazareth bore to the blond Scandinavian who adorned the Sunday School walls of my childhood. But it's difficult to communicate without pronouns, so we'll continue to follow tradition in using the forms *he*, *his*, *him* without imagining that God has a gender.

Genesis tells us that the universe comes from God. We will sketch some of the science that describes the process.

The Son. The second person in the Trinity, the Son, is the symbol used to identify Jesus, the Christ. A longer form of confession, the Athanasian Creed, emphasizes that the Son is eternal, rather than having come into existence two thousand years ago with the birth of Jesus.

Jesus is the incarnation of the Word. The Word was with God in the beginning. As God is the ground of being, the Word is the meaning of being. Being and meaning are inseparable.

Our discussion of meaning will have to distinguish the chemistry of the ordinary physical elements that make up our bodies from the software that animates them. The software is the pattern by which the elements are arranged and take on their special value. We are coming to understand the chemistry, but the pattern remains mysterious. The pattern is invisible but very real; it is intangible yet indestructible. The pattern of human life is the soul, and there is no evidence that it can't survive the decomposition of our bodies. The soul of Jesus, the incarnation of the meaning of being, is unique; his body was no more remarkable than yours or mine. The incarnation of the Word in human form is the central event of history, uniting, in a single instant, the human and the divine.

The Holy Spirit. God the Holy Spirit is a less visual symbol than the Father or the Son. The Spirit has most often been represented either as a dove or as tongues of flame. These are pictorial representations, less literal than a parent or a child, though those are also symbolic rather than strictly literal. The Spirit is the perceptible presence of God today, guiding us as individuals and as a church. The word *spirit* is closely related to the word *breath*, and when we are inspired we breathe in the spirit. As the Son is the meaning of being, the Spirit is the breath of being.

God communicates with us in a variety of ways, including prayer and sacraments. Scripture contains God's gradual revelation over the centuries. The revelation must be gradual as it cannot go beyond what people of the time can encompass. It certainly cannot be the record of what God dictated to scribes; that would reduce the inspired authors of scripture to mere stenographers, rather than the autonomous creatures God needs. Christ is the final revelation. But our understanding is not final; it can and must continue to grow.

The Trifurcated Deity

The Trinity has always been a difficult doctrine, as shown by the historic struggles to create a coherent creed. It is part of the doctrine itself that the Trinity is a mystery, not to be comprehended by any human. But each time Christianity severs itself from generally accepted knowledge, it sets up stumbling blocks to belief. We don't need to strain ourselves to believe that God experiences himself as trifurcated. Blood has been shed over this idea, but surely today it is enough that the concept of the Trinity is an organizing principle for our relationship with God. We experience God through his creation, of which we are a part; through his redemptive acts in healing our estrangement; and through his revelatory presence in our lives on a daily basis. These are the ways in which he is tangible and specific for us. We don't know how he experiences himself. There is enough about Christian doctrine that is inherently astounding and hard to believe. There is no need to invent difficulties. The Bible contains stories, like the creation myths of Genesis, that are clearly inventions intended to make a point. While recognizing their enormous beauty and value, we don't have to insist on treating such stories as historical documents.

The chapters that follow flesh out these ideas. The goal is to make sense of humankind's relationship to God while embracing scientific knowledge and insights arising from empirical observation and rational thinking. There is no attempt to prove any statement about God. Faith is the conviction of things *not* seen;[10] things that are seen – that can be proved – do not require faith.

But faith is not the acceptance of things we know to be false. That would be the definition of George Orwell's doublethink. God is not the White Queen, exhorting Alice to believe seven impossible things before breakfast. The existence of a conscious, loving, creative power on which our own existence depends is astounding, but it is not impossible: it does not contradict anything we know. If it seems implausible, we note (*pace* Laplace) that no alternative hypothesis is less implausible. We do not make fools of ourselves by choosing to believe.

---

10 Hebrews 11:1. All scriptural citations are from *The Holy Bible, New Revised Standard Version, New York, Oxford University Press, 1989*

SECTION 1:
The Ground of Being

We believe in one God, the Father, the Almighty,
maker of heaven and earth, of all that is, seen and unseen.

CHAPTER 1:
Priests, Scientists, and Priest-Scientists

W hy did God create us?"

The great theologian took my question seriously. I guess he thought it was a significant question, even though it was being asked by an insignificant undergraduate. His name was Paul Tillich and he was visiting Wagner College in the Spring of 1960. He was the principal speaker at Faith and Life Week, Wagner's Lenten observance, and his coming was a major event. He gave several talks and hosted question-and-answer sessions with faculty and students.

Professor Tillich was an impressive speaker. His lectures were so well-organized that my notes took form without any effort from me as a coherent outline of what he had said. At Q&A sessions he always answered in ordered paragraphs with no pause for reflection. But he smoked a pipe – in those days such behavior was not considered antisocial – which invariably went out while he answered. So when he wasn't talking he was relighting his pipe and possibly using the time to decide what he would say next.

I was more than a little nervous at the end of one of these sessions when I walked up to him and stammered out my question. After all, this was one of the premier theologians of the mid-twentieth century. I thought I might get a dismissive answer: "How should I know God's reasons?" But he didn't act annoyed or contemptuous – he was always kind in the days I saw him – and he seemed confident that he knew the answer. Without pausing to light his pipe, he told me that God was a creative principle and one couldn't picture him deciding, "Now I will create the universe and for this reason…"

That was good news and bad news. The good news was that I hadn't been annihilated. The bad news was that his answer was disturbing: in a sense it was no answer at all. I had thought I might hear some compelling reasons for creation. Instead Tillich seemed to be telling me that God created us because that's what God knows how to do. I now understand that he only indicated the answer rather than spelling it out. He published a more detailed and totally electrifying answer a few years later, but I didn't see it until a long time afterward.

Concepts of the Divine

Still, what Tillich told me that day in 1960 is a good place to start. God *is* a creative principle. We view him as the author of being. The Nicene Creed defines him as "maker…of all that is, seen and unseen." God is radically different from us and we should not expect to understand him fully, even though we are told he created us in his image.[11] But we have to try: that's the kind of creature a human being is. If we take God seriously it is natural to form concepts, at a human level, of what God intends for us and demands from us, and what we can expect from him. Despite the biblical injunction (in traditional translations) against images, Christianity is full of them. The human mind cannot contain literal concepts of the abyssal ground of being. Religions have no choice but to discuss their deities in terms that either reduce the god himself (or herself, as in the ancient goddess religions) to manageable size, or to admit that they are focusing on a comprehensible aspect of the incomprehensible. When Christians describe God in terms that are patriarchal (father), rural (shepherd), feudal (lord), royal (king), or even ornithological (dove), we form a concept we can grasp, and also one that can be depicted. The understanding that the Second Commandment forbids the making of an idol, not an image,[12] allowed an artistic history in painting and sculpture that made religion more accessible to millions.

Today patriarchy is out of style, and most of us are not rural, feudal, royalist, or ornithological, but the traditional symbols and concepts we grew up with continue to provide understanding, solace, and inspiration. At the same time we now have additional concepts to supplement that

11   Genesis 1:27

12   Exodus 20:4-6

tradition. Genesis describes the creation of the universe as taking six days. Modern cosmology, science's approach to the same question, says creation has taken fourteen billion years. But this only seems like a serious contradiction. "Six days" is not a core concept. The elapsed time is the least important part of the biblical creation myth. In its own terms Genesis is right to describe an act of loving creation culminating in the appearance of humankind. Science describes more details of the development of the universe, our planet, life, and culture, allowing theists to see the creator as the prime mover of a fourteen billion year process whose outline is at last beginning to be known. The myth exists to suggest to us a response to the divine gift. Faith allows us to live out that response.

Science is silent on the prime mover: it is a *spiritual* synthesis – a statement of faith – to link God to scientific cosmology. But there is no contradiction. As long as we don't try to wring scientific data out of creation myths, or spiritual values out of science, the myths and the science complement each other. The universe as we understand it has grown much larger than tradition imagined it. Why should anyone think that makes its creator smaller? We can see the soul, not as a mysterious weightless fluid but as the pattern that makes our mundane elements into something that with God's blessing is ultimately significant to the universe and beyond. Spiritual concepts gain substance for us when they can be seen in the light of what we learn from other ways of searching for truth.

Concepts of the divine have been important to the human race for a long time, probably about as long as there have been human concepts of anything. Atheism is a fairly new worldview; it was hardly possible until quite recently. As far as we know, animals other than humans are not equipped to ask questions about God. It has been said that the dogs who live with us consider us gods – my Golden Retriever seems to be an agnostic – but it is probably a sentimental error to think that a dog with his nose pressed against the car window is pining for a religious experience. What he wants is a romp, or possibly a dog biscuit, or in a perfect world, both. (On the other hand, perhaps his desire to be taken wherever we're going *is* a primitive religious yearning. The apostles expressed a similar wish to go with Jesus, even though they didn't know where he was going and didn't manage to stay the course.[13]) The point when members of our

---

13   John 13:36-38

species developed the ability to consider their relationships with gods is a pretty good definition of the dawn of the human race.

The Rational and the Numinous

Rudolph Otto[14] has discussed a transcendent, non-rational experience that he says is common to primitive and modern humans. Though not truly describable, it contains components of such experiences as dread, awe, and fascination. It may, in part, be analogous to the feeling of being helpless in the presence of a thunderstorm, or stunned by the beauty of a symphony, or enraptured before a great painting or sculpture. Otto calls it the experience of the numinous: that part of the holy which goes beyond the rational. It is a powerful, irresistible experience.

When I was a small child I had an experience of dread. I was on my front lawn, and a radio near an open window was playing a record called "The Littlest Angel." The story was about a child who died and went to Heaven, where he was a bit of a misfit. I guess he was not into harp music and it was the kind of Heaven where everyone played a harp. The narrator said the young angel could be forgiven if he took an illicit swing on the pearly gates, two or even three times, to relieve his boredom. And I was shocked. I have no idea how the rest of the story played out. I couldn't get past the fact that the kid was bored. If he was bored now, he would always be bored. After a year, a century, a billion centuries, he would be no closer to the end of his agony. The boredom would continue and would always get worse. For the first time I glimpsed eternity, and I was horrified. The horror felt by Tolstoy's Levin, described in the Introduction, must have been similar. Otto names horror as a component of the numinous experience. A well-known hymn declares,

> *When we've been there ten thousand years,*
> *Bright shining as the sun*

---

14 Otto, Rudolph, *The Idea of the Holy*, Second Edition, Translated by John W. Harvey, London, Oxford, New York, Oxford University Press, 1950 (First Edition published 1923)

We've no less days to sing God's praise
Than when we first begun

That could be heard as a threat. I had tiptoed up to the brink of the abyss.

Otto is saying that early humans found themselves at the edge of the abyss. He says the experience is "daemonic":

...it goes beyond all "conceiving", surpasses "understanding" and "reason", and consequently is "inapprehensible"

Primitive people had never heard of infinity, but they were experiencing mystery beyond fathoming. They couldn't opt for atheism. Captivated by their experience of the numinous, they quickly rationalized this experience through a belief in higher powers. But Otto says the numinous experience came first, before any sort of rational understanding. We can get an idea of their response from the discovery of religious items – yes, they were probably idols – among the earliest artifacts. When we started making anything of esthetic value with our hands, spiritually important objects appeared almost at once. These items seem to be the beginning of worship. They are markers of the emergence of humanity.

The question of God's nonexistence would hardly have arisen in a world so full of otherwise inexplicable mysteries. People saw the sun rise and set and were forced to synchronize their daily activities accordingly for almost the entire history of humanity: strong reliable artificial light has been available for less than two centuries. They saw lightning's devastation and heard thunder's roar, and humbly realized that they were in the presence of an irresistible power. They learned to survive on the basis of food that sprouted from the ground, and how to sow seed to increase the food supply. They saw infants delivered alive from their mothers, though it was many millennia before they realized how that numinous train of events was seeded, and many more before they began to understand the details of the process. In the early days, God the creative energy would have had to be female and apparently she was. Many goddess-mother figures from earliest human time have been found.

Humans had their numinous experiences in a context of rational concerns. They were faced with inexplicable fertility on the one hand and irresistible threats on the other: the unpredictable forces they encountered were enough to inspire an attempt to understand, to propitiate, to gain some measure of safety if not control. Maybe the grains could be made to grow where and when they were most needed. Maybe the spirit of the lightning could be appeased so that no more clan members would be incinerated. These were intensely practical matters. Early humans must have found it impossible to explain their universe without invoking creator gods. The sun was recognized as essential; it would have seemed suicidal not to commemorate this fact with ceremonies of worship.

Gods imagined for this purpose have to be multiple. If many different phenomena are to be organized in terms of their causative gods, there need to be many gods. One of the triumphs of science is its ability to organize disparate phenomena in terms of a limited number of basic concepts. Scientists speak of elegance. Their definition of the word doesn't have much to do with clothing fashions: elegance is the ability to explain a wide range of phenomena on the basis of a small number of assumptions. The late P.A.M. Dirac, a Nobel Prize winning physicist, felt that if a theory wasn't beautiful – more or less what we've called elegant – it was probably wrong. The development of monotheism represents a striking application of the principle of elegance to the spiritual domain. But it's a late development. Polytheism was the standard model for more than ninety percent of the history of religion.

Chaco Canyon

If Otto is right, earliest religion started with a response to numinous experience, which was rationalized in terms of gods of natural phenomena. This rationalization was a lot like science, whose purpose is to gain understanding. The ancient understanding fused science and religion, speaking in terms of gods who controlled natural phenomena. The supposed conflict between science and religion is a tragic modern development. In ancient times priests and scientists, if they weren't the same individuals, were allied in working toward the same goals. The scientific and the religious were closely intertwined and were central to the serious business of survival.

A few years ago I happened to see a documentary film[15] by Anna Sofaer about activities in Chaco Canyon. It struck me as an extraordinary demonstration of this mingling of the scientific and the spiritual at the center of an ancient civilization. The native Chacoan people, today sometimes referred to as Anasazi, are no longer there: Chaco Canyon is uninhabited. Scholars debate where they went and why – modern Pueblo people seem to be their descendants – but we know for certain that they left after completing a massive building project that took place between the ninth and twelfth centuries. In 850 C.E. there were only small clusters of subsistence farmers contending with short growing seasons, long harsh winters, and scarce water. Like much of New Mexico, Chaco is not reliably fertile. The subsistence farmers didn't leave much trace, but what happened next was far more impressive.

Over the next two and a half centuries the Chacoans constructed fourteen massive buildings of up to five stories, known as great houses. The largest building, Pueblo Bonito (as the Chacoan language was not recorded, modern names are used)[16] covers three acres and is the size of the Roman Coliseum. Since the necessary building materials were not available locally, 220,000 timbers were transported fifty to seventy miles by thousands of workers on foot. The Chacoans built roads in an area of 95,000 square miles and traded with people thousands of miles to the south.

When people build three-acre houses we presume they wish to house a lot of people. But that doesn't seem to have been the case at Chaco. The three thousand rooms of the great houses had interesting architectural features, of which one in particular stands out: many had

15 "The Mystery of Chaco Canyon", ©1999, The Solstice Project, A Presentation of South Carolina ETV, Written by Anna Sofaer and Matt Dibbel, Produced and Directed by Anna Sofaer, Narrated by Robert Redford

16   Fagan, Brian, *Chaco Canyon: Archaeologists Explore the Lives of an Ancient Society,* New York NY, Oxford University Press, 2005 describes the naming in 1849 of several archaeological sites, including Pueblo Pintado among others, by Carravahal, the Mexican guide to an exploratory party headed by James Hervey Simpson.

no doorways. Chetro Ketl, for example, had six hundred rooms closed off from the central plaza, the outside, and each other. Cartoonists draw pictures of buffoons painting themselves into corners – it's a traditional staple of comic art – but in real life who would build a room that could not be entered? The most plausible explanation is that the rooms were never occupied: they weren't rooms in the usual sense. Perhaps they were structural elements in buildings primarily intended not as dwellings, but as monuments. This suggestion is supported by the fact that there is no sign of mass occupation in the great houses: few hearths, few burial remains, little evidence that the huge mounds near the houses ever contained the organic matter typical of trash heaps. Instead of the ten thousand people the buildings were large enough to house there may have been only a relative handful. In this view the building project at Chaco was not devoted to a center of population, but to a center of something larger. The buildings are reminiscent in their way of the cathedrals that emerged in Europe from the partnership of architects and religious authorities.

The Fajada Butte Observatory

Rising steeply from the south end of the canyon, Fajada Butte is the site of fascinating clues to what the great houses were for.[17] It is a complicated picture, suggesting a merging of spirituality with impressive scientific accomplishment. It's worth taking a little time to understand it, though the point I'm trying to make does not require that you follow every detail. If you find yourself confused reading about it, imagine the scientific intelligence the Chacoans must have applied to developing it!

On a ledge next to a cliff wall near the top of the butte three

---

17 Sofaer AP and Sinclair RM, "Astronomical Markings at Three Sites on Fajada Butte." *From* Carlson JB and Judge WJ, editors, *Astronomy and Ceremony in the Prehistoric Southwest, Maxwell Museum of Anthropology, Anthropological Papers,* No. 2, 1983. This paper and the five following may be viewed online at www.solsticeproject.org

large, flat stones stand on end, looking like oversized tombstones. The people of Chaco used these tombstones to mark the principal events of the solar year and of the much longer lunar cycles. The sun and the moon, phenomena of the greatest importance to the Chacoans, were captured in this one simple construction, as accurately today as eight hundred years ago. This was all accomplished without written records and despite the fact that a Chacoan's adult life would rarely cover more than two of the moon's long cycles. The construction was simple, but the scientific and spiritual ideas it depended on were profound. Fajada Butte was a center, perhaps *the* center, of scientific and spiritual seeking in a very substantial region.

The focus of the construction is the stone slabs, each six to ten feet high and weighing more than a ton.[18] Picture them: they rest on the ledge like giant slices of salami, with their broad faces a few inches apart and their thin edges leaning against the cliff wall behind them. Since they do not touch, they form a giant comb. They were originally placed in the general area by natural causes, but it is very probable that their positions and shapes have been adjusted by human agents.

Most of the time no sunlight gets through the narrow spaces between the slabs, and the cliff wall behind them is in shadow. Shortly before noon, however, there is a brief time when narrow shafts of sunlight slip between the slabs and reach the wall. For a few minutes or a couple of hours, depending on the season, two beams of light get through and each produces a dagger-shaped spot on the wall. These have come to be called "sun daggers." As the sun moves in the sky the sun daggers travel in an almost straight line downward along the wall. On a given day the daggers move vertically. When they appear on the next day the daggers are shifted a little to the left or right, but again move vertically. The transformation from primarily horizontal daily motion of the sun to vertical motion of the sun daggers results from the precisely calibrated tilt and curvature of the stone slabs. It's not easy to picture, but it happens.

---

18   Sofaer AP, Zinser V, and Sinclair RM, "A Unique Solar Marking Construct." *Science* vol 206, number 4416, October 19, 1979, pp 283-291

The Writing On the Wall

The Chacoans arranged things so that the positions of the sun daggers have cosmic significance. To do this they created a petroglyph: they carved – the technical term is "pecked" – two spirals into the cliff face. These were not superficial scratches: they are still clearly visible today. The spirals are sketched in Figure 1. The noontime positions of the sun daggers on these spirals mark the principal days of the solar year. On the day of the summer solstice – the longest, brightest day of the year – the right-hand sun dagger passes through the center of the large spiral, as shown in Figure 1a. (The left-hand dagger is seen only fleetingly on this day and does not fall on the spiral.) Then as the days and months go by the positions of both daggers gradually move to the right. The left-hand dagger enters the arena and on the autumnal equinox, halfway between the summer and winter solstices, it passes through the center of the smaller spiral, as shown in Figure 1b. With the further passage of time both daggers move farther to the right. At the winter solstice – the shortest, darkest day of the year – they bracket the large spiral, "holding it empty of light" in the authors' description. This position is shown in Figure 1c. At this point the day-to-day movement of the daggers reverses: now each day the daggers are shifted a little to the left. They pass through the spring equinox, in which the pattern resembles that of the autumn equinox, and on back to the summer solstice and the next reversal.

There are only two solstices and two equinoxes each year. The Chacoans did not have written language. They nevertheless managed to adjust the massive stone slabs – they probably had to perfect the shapes of their edges – and to place the spirals so as to create an accurate calendar to identify the main checkpoints of the year. And it's a durable calendar, still readable and accurate after eight hundred years.

There's a lot more[19] and it doesn't get simpler. The moon appears

---

19 Sofaer A, Sinclair RM, and Doggett LE, "Lunar Markings on Fajada Butte, Chaco Canyon, New Mexico." *From* Aveni AF, editor, *Archaeoastronomy in the New World*, pp169-186, Cambridge

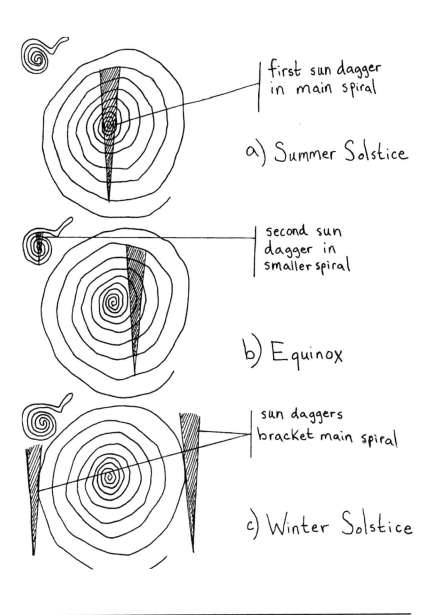

first sun dagger in main spiral

a) Summer Solstice

second sun dagger in smaller spiral

b) Equinox

sun daggers bracket main spiral

c) Winter Solstice

Figure 1. The sun daggers' positions on the petroglyph at Fajada Butte. (a) At summer solstice the first dagger is centered on the larger spiral. (b) At the autumnal equinox the second dagger is centered on the smaller spiral. (The position of the first dagger on the larger spiral has no known significance.) (c) At the winter solstice the two daggers bracket but do not illuminate the larger spiral. The configuration at the spring equinox is the same as is shown in (b).

to move generally from east to south to west each night, while rising to its zenith and descending to its setting position. The sun's motion each day is similar, but the moon's pattern of movement is much more complex than the sun's. One reason is that the moon's declination – a measure of how high it appears at its zenith – varies much more than the sun's. Moonrise can take place at many positions from northeast to southeast, and these positions vary in cycles.

The moon's pattern begins with a *short* cycle of approximately twenty-seven days. (Don't confuse the short cycle with the cycle of the moon's phases, whose length is closer to twenty-nine days.) At the beginning of the short cycle the moon rises somewhere in the northeast. As the cycle progresses the point of rising moves southward – in other words from the northeast toward the southeast – so that thirteen or fourteen days later the moon rises in its most southerly position in that short cycle. After this the motion of the moonrise position reverses direction and moonrise moves back toward the northeast. At the end of the cycle there's another reversal: day by day, moonrise begins to move southward again, and a new short cycle starts.

The short cycle isn't too hard to observe and follow, but it is only the beginning of the complexity. The entire short cycle takes place over and over in different positions in the sky. Each short cycle contributes a single point, called the *limit*, to the definition of the *long* cycle. Think of the hour hand on a clock advancing one hour each time the minute hand goes all the way around. The limit point is the most northerly moonrise point in a short cycle. The succession of limit points, one from each short cycle, traces the long cycle. The long cycle is aptly named: it plays out over almost two decades as the succession of limit points moves slowly to the south and then back to the north. The point in the long cycle where the moon rises farthest of all to the north is called the minor standstill. Years later, at what is called the major standstill, moonrise reaches the most southerly of all the limit points.

Archaeoastronomy in the New World, pp169-186, Cambridge University Press

So, long before the Chacoans or anyone else were around to observe it, moonrise was following a complicated pattern. Very careful measurements are required to show that the major standstill and the minor standstill are separated by 9.3 years: it takes that long to go from minor standstill to major standstill and another 9.3 years to go back to minor standstill. If a total of 18.6 years is required to see the full long cycle once, it must have taken generations to study and plot it accurately. A Chacoan's adult life would usually have extended through no more than two long cycles.

But even without written records the Chacoans analyzed all this and measured the length of the long cycle. Then they managed to record it using the same three stone slabs and Fajada Butte petroglyph. There are no daggers this time, and the observation is not made when the moon is at its highest. Instead, the moon as it rises shines its light obliquely behind the nearest slab and casts a shadow on the cliff wall. At minor standstill the edge of this shadow falls across the center of the larger spiral petroglyph: the same spot marked by the sun at summer solstice. At major standstill the shadow has moved from the center to the outer edge of the spiral. The spiral contains 9½ turns, very nearly (within about 2%) analogous to the 9.3 years required for the moon to move from minor to major standstill. One comb of rocks and one petroglyph are able to record both solar and lunar milestone events, in a remarkable scientific tour de force.

Even if you haven't followed all the complexities of the solar-lunar observatories, wrap your mind around this: with three stone slabs and a few pecks on the wall, the Chacoans recorded the major solar milestones and a lunar cycle of over eighteen years, in an installation we can observe and marvel at today.

The Spiritual Dimension

Why was all this science worth the effort? Agriculture was the basis of their civilization, a civilization that could not have been supported in its complex form by hunter-gatherers. There were important religious observances associated with the seasons as they related to milestones in the agricultural process – planting, harvesting, and so forth – and the scientifically impressive Fajada Butte observatory presumably supported these spiritually essential observances. Judging by modern Pueblo cultures, the moon also had great ceremonial significance, and the Chacoans were interested in integrating the sun and the moon.

We note that the science is in immediate proximity to a spiritual statement. Another petroglyph, ten meters from the observatory, declares a close relationship between the sun and Pueblo Bonito, the largest great house. This petroglyph is sketched in Figure 2a. The horizontal and vertical lines and rough semicircle resemble the floor plan of Pueblo Bonito, which is sketched in outline in Figure 2b. It has a straight wall that is oriented very accurately east-west, a semicircular wall that meets the straight wall at each end, and a north-south wall that bisects the east-west wall. It also has a great kiva in the position of the small circle. The kiva was a ceremonial gathering place, a center of religious observance. Pueblo Bonito's great kiva is represented by a drilled hole in the petroglyph. There is no doubt that the lower part of the petroglyph is intended to identify Pueblo Bonito.

The rest of the petroglyph makes a statement about the great house. The arrow points to the center of the spiral immediately above. We recall that the petroglyph of Figure 1 associates the center of a spiral with the dagger projected by the sun. (The butte actually contains eight associations of spirals with the motion of the sun; there is more on Fajada Butte than we can discuss here.) The north-south wall of Pueblo Bonito points directly south to the noonday sun at summer solstice; the arrow in the petroglyph commemorates this orientation. The petroglyph, the Pueblo, and the sun are tightly linked in their celebration of the cosmos. The observatory petroglyph records and merges the chief movements of the sun and moon: a major scientific achievement. The adjacent petroglyph affirms the relationship between the sun and the largest great house: a spiritual declaration.

Figure 2. (a) The petroglyph depicting Pueblo Bonito. The bottom portion of the petroglyph outlines the shape of Pueblo Bonito, and includes a drilled hole (the black dot). The north-south wall is incorporated into an arrow pointing at the center of the spiral above it. (b) The outline and overall floor plan of Pueblo Bonito, including an east-west wall segment (the right-hand portion of the south wall), an intersecting north-south wall, and a roughly semicircular wall, resembling the petroglyph. The great kiva, sketched as a small circle, occupies the same relative position as the drilled hole in the petroglyph. The pueblo is accurately aligned to the cardinal points, as indicated in the sketch.

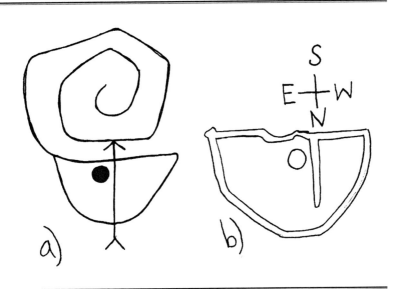

The Planned City

We have spoken so far of basic science, without any engineering applications (apart from the engineering challenge of positioning and shaping one ton rock slabs with exquisite accuracy.) But there is impressive engineering in the great houses of Chaco,[20] and it also marches in the service of religious observance. Sighting along the east-west wall of Pueblo Bonito is equivalent to following the movement of the sun at summer solstice, and Pueblo Bonito is far from being the only great house with an orientation related to the

20 Sofaer A, "The Primary Architecture of the Chacoan Culture: A Cosmographic Expression." *From* Morrow BH and Price VB, editors, *Anasazi Architecture and American Design*, Albuquerque NM, University of New Mexico Press, 1997

path of the sun, or the moon, or both. In fact the entire complex is very carefully integrated; it can be seen as an example of prehistoric city planning. Four buildings have major walls oriented to the solar equinox, one to the solstice, two to the major lunar standstill, and five to the minor lunar standstill. The diagonal lines within the buildings are also significant in some cases: three buildings have major walls and diagonals oriented to both the sun and the moon.

The layout of the great houses relative to each other has further significance. The east-west sight line from Pueblo Bonito passes precisely through Chetro Ketl. The line from Pueblo Alto to Tsin Kletsin is in a precise north-south direction, and this line is bisected by the line from Pueblo Bonito to Chetro Ketl. These four great houses thus form the basis of a gigantic compass, with the cardinal points marked by massive buildings.

Many of the lines connecting great houses are in the direction of either the major or minor lunar standstill. In all, seven of the great houses are accurately aligned to lunar standstill positions, and almost all of them are related to other great houses by lines along these same directions. Kin Bineola and Pueblo Pintado, eleven and seventeen miles away and not visible from Chetro Ketl, are related to it by the directions of the rising and setting moon at minor standstill. Many of the houses that are aligned are far apart and separated by buttes and other natural features, so they are not in visual communication. The overall alignment of the great houses with respect to the sun, the moon, and each other cannot be seen from any one building – the Chacoans did not use helicopters – but apparently was present in the minds of the people, or at least some of their scientific and religious leaders.

Yet another engineering accomplishment focusing on a cardinal direction is the Great North Road[21] which, after a two-mile feeder segment from Pueblo Alto, runs due north (within one half degree) for ten miles. The road – actually two and in some cases four parallel roads very close

21 Sofaer A, Marshall MP, Sinclair RM, "The Great North Road: a Cosmographic Expression of the Chaco Culture of New Mexico." *From* Aveni AF, editor, *World Archaeoastronomy*, pp365-376, Cambridge University Press

together – averages thirty feet in width, more than a modern two-lane road. This might have been useful for movement of large wagons pulled by draft animals or even by humans, but the Chacoans didn't have draft animals and they didn't have wagons. They walked. The road was thus far wider than the Chacoans needed. It didn't go anywhere of much commercial importance and its direction was unaffected by topological features. There is evidence of ceremonial activity with breaking of pots. Pots were often broken, and thus rendered unusable by humans, when they were to become sacrificial offerings. There is little evidence of commerce or of encampment along the road, certainly nothing commensurate with the effort put into engineering and construction.

The road just went north. Considered only in the utilitarian sense it was a little-traveled road to nowhere. But it clearly had a deeper meaning.

The Center Place

Beyond science, the sun and moon were objects of intense spiritual significance to the Chacoans. According to Anna Sofaer:

In many Pueblo traditions, the people emerged in the north from the worlds below and traveled to the south in search of the sacred middle place…a center around which the recurring solar and lunar cycles revolve. Chaco Canyon may have been such a center place.

The Great North Road was a straight path in the traditional direction toward the sipapu, the point of emergence of the original people from the worlds below. Unification of the sun and moon in a single petroglyph was a feat of spiritual importance to the Chacoans. It was also a massive technical challenge, combining decades of observations with brilliant conception and execution of the positioning of the stone slabs. It is clear that the best available scientific talent was devoted to the creation of this versatile arrangement of rock slabs and pecks in the side of the butte, with its profound connections to the heavens. The spiritual dimension is further emphasized by the adjacent petroglyph commenting on the largest of the great houses. Chaco was a hallowed place, and science took a leading role in its hallowing.

So if the great houses were not population centers, it is more than plausible that they were spiritual centers. Further support for this idea comes from excavation of the mounds near the houses, which were found to contain not garbage, but thousands of broken pots, again suggesting ceremonial activity. It appears, then, that science and religion were united in the quest for understanding, power, and control; the scientific leaders of Chaco were either identical with the spiritual leaders or were closely allied with them. Over two and a half centuries, the Chacoan priest-scientists conceived and constructed a vast complex unifying the cosmic center with the spiritual center of their civilization.

The project in Chaco Canyon was important enough to be worth a very substantial proportion of the Chacoan gross domestic product. Religion and science – mystic knowledge and painstaking research – were one. Priests and scientists were in the same business: they were the truth-seekers. The Chacoans would have stared in amazement at anyone who suggested that priests and scientists occupied warring camps.

By the way, we have no full explanation for the last act in the epic. Having completed this enormous project over a span of ten generations, the people of Chaco Canyon sealed the buildings. They removed the roofs from the ceremonial kivas and burned them. Then they departed, possibly because the scarcity of water had become chronic, possibly for reasons we will never know.

Apparently their work was done.

CHAPTER 2:
The Schism

The monumental achievements at Chaco are a fascinating study. Why is this story relevant to our considerations? Because the situation there is just one example of a relationship that prevailed for a long time. What was true of Chaco Canyon and Fajada Butte had been and continued to be true elsewhere: from thousands of years before the peak activity of the Chacoans until a few centuries after, the unity of religion and science in the search for truth was the rule. In those days no one was arguing that science proved that religion was nonsense or that religion must put a lid on scientific endeavor. Then the relationship changed. Step by step a foundation was laid for alternative scientific worldviews that appeared to contradict, rather than fortify, sacred teachings. Instead of unity in a society characterized by priest-scientists, a fault line began to develop between the priestly and scientific functions.

Nicolaus Copernicus (1473-1543), Johannes Kepler (1571-1630), and Galileo Galilei (1564-1642), were among the earliest to disturb the traditional structure. Their scientific writings were not intended to challenge the religious order – though these men were all more or less idealistic, none of them was suicidal – but the Church was quick to sense and to resent the threat they presented. The first battleground was the same subject that had so inspired the Chacoans: the view of the heavens.

The Cosmological Conundrum
The objects visible to the naked eye – the sun, the moon, the stars, and the planets – are God's most spectacular creations. The Bible talks about their coming into existence and their behavior. Scripture states that on one occasion Joshua gave orders to the sun and the sun obeyed:

Joshua spoke to the Lord; and he said in the sight of Israel, "Sun, stand still at Gibeon, and Moon, in the valley of Aijalon." And the sun stood still, and the moon stopped, until the nation took vengeance on their enemies.[22]

All this made the sky the province of the Church. Celestial objects provided by God were understood to be unsullied, perfect. And they had grave import for earthly events: the subjects of astronomy and astrology were pretty much the same. Astrology was *really* important: it was a key input to decision-making at every level up to the imperial. As the Church placed mankind at the heart of God's creation, and placed itself in control of mankind's relationship with God, it placed Earth at the center of all celestial motions: the universe revolved around Earth, around humankind, around God... and around the Church.

The Church was certain that Earth was stationary:

You have set the earth upon its foundations, so that it shall never move at any time.[23]

The Chacoans never heard of the European church but they would have understood this concept of stable, immobile centrality. As Anna Sofaer wrote, Chaco Canyon may have been regarded as a center place and commemorated as such by the petroglyphs and by the monumental architecture.

In Rome, as in Chaco Canyon, Earth's position at the center had profound religious and political significance. Heretical suggestions that the actual arrangement was different could lead to questioning of the Church's central role and ultimate authority. And the claim that the earth was at the center was in fact quite consistent with most of what was observed. Then as now the vast majority of celestial objects marched predictably across the sky. You can see them today if you get far enough from urban light pollution: as observed from the northern hemisphere, constellations and individual bright stars all describe counterclockwise circles around the north star, Polaris.

The picture you see suggests that the stars are attached to a huge hollow sphere surrounding Earth and rotating around an axle

---

22 Joshua 10:12-13

23 Psalms 104:5

connecting the North Pole to the north star. Of course today we know that axle to be the axis of our planet's rotation. While Earth daily spins 360 degrees on its axis, the hollow sphere holding the stars appears to rotate a little more than 360 degrees. We now understand that the difference results from the annual revolution of Earth around the sun. The bright points of light are the so-called fixed stars. The southern hemisphere has no equivalent to Polaris, but the stars move in circles – clockwise this time – about an empty point in the sky at the other end of the same axle. The view won't have changed noticeably since the time of Copernicus. Five hundred years is nothing to a star.

If the sun, the moon, and the fixed stars had been the entire display, there would have been little need for Copernicus. But a few deviant specks in the sky moved erratically in a way that showed that they were not attached to the same sphere as the fixed stars. Sometimes they would even move backwards – clockwise in the northern hemisphere – a phenomenon called retrograde motion. These objects, called planets or wanderers, could not be ignored: astrology is for the most part based on the positions of the planets against the background of the fixed stars. Planets produced the bulk of the workload for astronomers; the fixed stars were easy to understand. In terms of the big picture, it was obvious (though false) that the celestial display rotated about Earth.

At the same time, the important astrological business of predicting the positions of planets could not easily be accomplished on the basis of the simple model of an Earth-centered sphere. It was vital to predict these positions because hardly anyone was paid for academic studies of the heavens. Astronomers made their livings as astrologers, casting horoscopes for rich patrons. To help them get the job done they invented tortured mental pictures and performed arduous computations of cycles and epicycles – imaginary wheels spinning on axles attached to the rims of other spinning wheels – so as to predict retrograde motion. Back when there were no computers, a computation like that was a backbreaking chore.

Nobody really believed in the clockwork of epicycles and the rest of this cosmic machinery. The job of these inventions was to "save the phenomenon": to produce a mental picture from which to calculate motions in agreement with those observed. The model did make it possible to accomplish this…more or less. A better picture was needed to obtain simpler, more accurate computations without postulating implausible machinery.

The Copernican Solution

The improvements to the picture took place in steps. First, Copernicus proposed a computational approach based on a radically different worldview. His picture was heliocentric: the sun was the center about which Earth and the planets traveled in circular orbits. The conceptual leap was enormous and heretical; Copernicus risked his life to make this suggestion. Earth no longer immobile, but moving around the sun! On the other hand, the Copernican scheme, while it wasn't perfect, made calculations simpler – no more need for epicycles – and more accurate. The Copernican system was also more plausible. Even before Isaac Newton (1642 or 1643 – 1727) unified cosmology with earthly mechanics, the picture of planets including Earth orbiting the sun did more than save the phenomenon. It made sense where epicycles did not.

A few decades after Copernicus, Kepler made crucial further refinements, including most significantly a change in the shape of the orbits of the planets. Instead of a circle, he postulated that an ellipse – an elongated circle, sort of an egg shape – would be more accurate. He showed that this approach could make the calculations match what was observed, but it also deepened the theological risk, as an ellipse was less "perfect" than a circle. Kepler himself, with childlike honesty and candor, described the elliptical orbits he postulated as "ugly." But the elliptical orbits of Kepler allowed the heliocentrism of the Copernican scheme to work much better. The combination made orbital calculations simpler and far more accurate.

Finally a clear demonstration that the Earth-centered view was flawed came from Kepler's contemporary Galileo, who used the recently invented telescope to observe satellites revolving around the planet Jupiter. This "Starry Messenger" (the title of his monograph on the subject) demonstrated that there were objects that did not revolve around Earth. The weight of evidence for the Copernican view, with Kepler's elliptical orbits, gradually became overwhelming, though the Church's capitulation on this point was made final only in the late twentieth century. Thus a computational simplification was associated with a fundamental paradigm shift.

The Ecclesiastical Reaction

The Church was not grateful. An enormous theological price was incurred for the paradigm shift that led to the computational improvements. It was bad enough that the orbital shape went from a "perfect" circle to an "ugly" ellipse. The more fundamental outrage was the removal of Earth from immobility at the center of the universe. Humankind became what we now know ourselves to be: passengers on an orbiting peripheral object rather than the geometrical focus of creation. The Church could not know specifically, but might guess in general terms, that someone would eventually describe our world in such unflattering terms as these:

Far out in the uncharted backwaters of the unfashionable end of the Western Spiral arm of the Galaxy lies a small unregarded yellow sun. Orbiting this at a distance of roughly ninety-eight million miles is an utterly insignificant little blue-green planet..."[24]

The planet described was Earth! This slap in the face was intolerable. We humans naturally are certain that we live on a *big* planet surrounded by tiny specks in the sky. That's what we see when we look out the window. We emphatically do not feel that we occupy an utterly insignificant planet orbiting an unregarded sun.

The Church rejected the paradigm shift of Copernicus, seeing a clear threat to its own privileged position, like that of the Chacoan priest-scientists, at the center of civilization and power. The Church

---

24 Adams, Douglas, *The Hitchhiker's Guide to the Galaxy,* Crown Publishers, Inc., New York NY, 1979

insisted that it was the single supreme authority. Science could explain things that did not impinge on doctrine, but must defer whenever Church fathers saw the possibility of a conflict. People must be taught that the home of humankind was at the center of the universe, because the Church interpreted the Bible as saying it was so. If the view through a telescope, or a calculation of planetary orbits, contradicted the traditional teaching, these observations or calculations must be suppressed as damaging to the minds of the faithful. That's why so many pious bureaucrats refused to look through Galileo's telescope. The universe was a perfect structure, created by God in a few days as a home for his children. If any deviation were allowed there was no telling where it could lead.

The Church had muscle and it used it relentlessly. Galileo was forced to recant under threat of torture, whatever he may have muttered under his breath.[25] Science would have to know its place: no longer a comrade to religion, but a subordinate that must abandon aspirations above its station. Still, as long-term developments demonstrated, the genie was out of the bottle. The Church eventually apologized to Galileo – three hundred and fifty years after his death.

The Paleontological Threat: Darwin

At this point, no one – certainly not Copernicus, Kepler, or Galileo – was proposing to remove God from creation; no one yet dared to suggest *that* much of a paradigm shift. Yet these pioneers had led the way to a slippery slope, even if they were not ready for the full toboggan ride. More direct threats arose later, most famously with the work of Charles Darwin (1809-1882). In 1831, having just finished his university course as a divinity student, Darwin sailed as an unpaid naturalist on the five-year voyage of HMS *Beagle*. The *Beagle*'s charter was to survey the coasts of South America and the Pacific islands. Darwin's work was a sideline but it's all that we now remember about the *Beagle*.

---

25 The tradition is that he said, "Eppur si muove" meaning "It still moves." There's no way of knowing, since if he had said it loud enough to be heard he would have been silenced for good.

Darwin, though a volunteer, took his duties seriously. He kept voluminous notes of his observations and sent specimens to scientific colleagues back home. And the specimens contained a bombshell. Among them were the remains of thirty-one finches from the Galapagos Islands. No ornithological expert, Darwin was surprised on his return to England to be told that his finches included thirteen distinct species, distinguished by the sizes and shapes of their beaks. Each species was adapted to a particular food. One with a large beak crushed and ate large seeds. Another with a narrow beak fed on insects. Yet another could puncture the skins of seabirds with its sharp beak and drink their blood. There was even a species that shaped a pointed instrument like a thorn or twig into a tool to pry grubs from dead branches, feeding on the natural prey of woodpeckers. This prey was available to finches because they didn't have to compete with woodpeckers. Isolated from the mainland, the islands boasted no woodpeckers.

The evidence led Darwin to question the conventional view that God had placed each species, complete with its adaptations to the environment, where it would thrive. "Seeing this gradation and diversity of structure in one small, intimately related group of birds," he proposed, "one might really fancy that from an original paucity of birds in this archipelago, one species had been taken and modified for different ends." Apart from their beaks the finch species were practically identical. Looking at them, it would be reasonable to infer that their beaks developed in response to the needs of their various feeding strategies, not that the finches were placed in their final forms on the Galapagos Islands.

The mechanism for this adaptive process was natural selection, the key process in the evolution of species. In conditions of scarcity more organisms are born than can survive and reproduce. And conditions of scarcity are the norm, as conditions of plenty naturally lead to high rates of birth and survival, to overpopulation, and before long to scarcity. (This may have been part of what led to the exodus from Chaco Canyon.) The competition for food is so fierce that small advantages, providing a statistical increase in the chance of surviving, become decisive. Among birds that feed on large seeds possession of a large beak provides an advantage: a slight increase in the probability of surviving and reproducing. If one flock of finches happened to feed on large seeds, those with larger beaks would tend to be more successful. And among the offspring of this generation of big-beaks, the individuals with the largest beaks of all tended to win the next round of the competition. So over the generations, finches that fed on large seeds developed larger and larger beaks, to the point where they became a separate species. In the same way, birds that ate insects found a different beak configuration to be a competitive advantage and gradually evolved toward narrow beaks. The large-beaked finches and the narrow-beaked finches lived on different food supplies, so they were not direct competitors.

These were not the only facts suggesting evolution. Additional evidence was found in the form of sequences of fossils showing that new species appeared in the same place as defunct predecessors. The active species were anatomically related to extinct species they replaced. The evolutionary process goes forward in steps. Though not every step is found in the fossil record, there is enough evidence to trace the progression toward the present occupiers of the site. The insight provided by the adapted finches, combined with fossils demonstrating the development of species through the ages, established the concept that natural selection causes new species to arise from those that came before them. It made perfect sense to Darwin the scientist. Darwin the graduate in divinity recognized that some people would not be happy to hear it.

The voyage of the *Beagle* ended in 1836. Darwin published uncontroversial scientific accounts of some of his observations, but did not publish *On the Origin of Species by Means of Natural Selection* until 1859, twenty-three years later. He was well aware of the hornet's nest he was stirring up, and apparently was made physically ill by the associated stress. He wrote, "The general conclusion at which I have slowly been driven from a directly opposite conviction is that species are mutable and that allied species are co-descendants of common stocks. I know how much I open myself, to reproach, for such a conclusion, but I have at least honestly and deliberately come to it."

Darwin's nervousness was well-founded. Clerical opposition to his position was fierce, based on the conventional notion that God personally equipped each species for the requirements of its environment: gills for a fish, wings for a bird, large beaks for a seed-cracker, and so forth. But it was difficult to square thirteen species of finch, all closely related and differing mainly in their beaks, with the conventional picture; why would God need so many kinds of finch? *The Descent of Man* and *Selection in Relation to Sex*, both published in 1871, completed the insult to conventional religious thinking by emphasizing humankind's similarities to the great apes.

From the churchly perspective things had gone from bad to much worse. Copernicus's heliocentric worldview, Kepler's elliptical orbits, and Galileo's starry messenger were far-off and abstract, their implications profound but subtle. Indeed they are widely accepted today by even the most fundamentalist religious sects. But Darwin's insights continue to create passionate controversy. Bad enough to think of Earth as a speck within the universe. But at least humans were unique, qualitatively different from anything else that breathed. Now the Garden of Eden was to be replaced by a view of Man as an ape who had lost his fur! For the first time, the shape of a new, godless paradigm could be discerned. Proofs of the existence of God had been demonstrations of reasoning power and wit, scholars proving to each other what few doubted. After Darwin serious doubt was possible: if we descended naturally from earlier primates, divine intervention might not be required. In this setting it was possible for religion to see science as a demonic enemy.

The Geological Threat: Hutton

Evolution was the most widely recognized threat to acceptance of God, but not the first. Darwin carried with him on the *Beagle* a book about the research of the geologist James Hutton (1726-1797). Hutton, a prominent figure in the Scottish Enlightenment and colleague of such men as Adam Smith, David Hume, and Benjamin Franklin, thought deeply about the development of the earth and came to the conclusion that it had resulted from natural processes playing out over a very long time. This placed him in profound conflict with the six-day timetable in Genesis. Further, it implied that the earth must be very old. But a very old earth was impossible because the age of the earth was known definitively from the research of Bishop James Ussher (1581-1656), who had calculated it using an unimpeachable source. Working from recorded lifetimes in the Old Testament, he was able to determine that the Creation occurred on the night of October 22-23 in 4004 B.C.E. So on that date in Autumn of 1996, Earth proudly celebrated its six thousandth birthday, according to Ussher's chronology.

Even though the answer was right there in the book, Hutton didn't believe it: he did not feel he could rely on the Bible to work out our planet's age. Instead he observed the earth itself, and reached some radical conclusions. As described in John McPhee's book, *Annals of the Former World*,[26] Hutton presented his findings to the Royal Society in 1785, stating that the land we see today is not the original surface of the earth. In former times, he announced, a different surface existed and supported plant and animal life. The present land was formed at the bottom of the ocean during those former times, and was consolidated and raised to the surface by extreme heat in the lower depths. Hutton concluded that the process of forming and raising the present land mass had required a long time, and that the formation of the previous surface land had required a comparably long time. There was no way of telling how many cycles of formation and raising of new surface land had occurred. The total time would, in any case, be far longer than Ussher's forty centuries from the beginning to the birth of Jesus, and eighteen more to Hutton's time.

Hutton felt sure that Earth must be a great deal older than Ussher had calculated. Searching for clear evidence he found a revealing rock formation near Jedburgh in southern Scotland. A mass of vertically oriented schist supported a horizontal mass of sandstone. Such a formation – a great many are known – is now called an angular

---

26 McPhee, John, *Annals of the Former World*, New York, Farrar, Straus and Giroux, 1998

unconformity because the masses lie at an angle to each other. Schist is basically a sedimentary rock, initially formed as sandstone by deposition of material floating in water and subsequently changed by contact with hot material coming up from Earth's core. When you see sedimentary rock it often appears tilted, but it can't have been laid down that way. The material collects in successive layers on the bottom of a body of water, so any sedimentary rock is initially laid down in horizontal sheets. Any time sedimentary rock appears at an orientation other than horizontal, that is proof that the entire rock mass has actually been rotated, or tipped, at least once after its horizontal deposition. The schist at Jedburgh was an extreme example. It had been rotated through a ninety degree angle: stood on its edge by inexorable geological processes. (Even more extreme examples are known; rock formations have been turned upside down by successive rotations.) Over the years after the Jedburgh schist was rotated it was covered by the sandstone mass, which in turn was topped by soil where trees later grew and people and animals lived.

But while most trees grow relatively quickly, geological processes are slow. A gigantic rock formation is not rotated through ninety degrees in a few years. We now know that the process typically involves enormous land masses moving ponderously together until one of them buckles and a portion is rotated and raised up. Sometimes a formation experiences two or more successive rotations. Land masses this large move slowly. Whole continents move thousands of miles, but this occurs over geologic time spans: millions of years. There is no mountain on Earth that occupied a different position from its present one at any time in living memory or indeed within historical time. The only record of a phenomenon like the angular unconformity at Jedburgh is the slowly evolving geologic record. No other record goes back far enough.

Hadrian's Wall

Hutton didn't know about the motion of continents, but he could point to other signs that the Jedburg unconformity was old. McPhee points out that Hutton was familiar with Hadrian's Wall, which the

Romans built in the second century C.E. for protection from the barbarians. It runs eighty miles across the width of Britain from the Atlantic Ocean to the North Sea. Hadrian's Wall tells us something about the relationship between geologic time and historical time. The wall was sixteen centuries old in Hutton's day – more than a quarter of Bishop Ussher's figure for the entire age of the earth – and while superficial features like towers had crumbled, the integrity of its basic structure could be seen to be largely preserved after all that time. It certainly hadn't been rotated or tipped. Sixteen centuries, it could be seen, represents historical time, not geologic time: not long enough for significant geologic change to occur. It was clear that the cataclysmic changes visible in the angular unconformity near Jedburgh must have required many times sixteen centuries. The successive processes that produced those changes could never have been accommodated in the fifty-eight centuries between Ussher's date for Creation and Hutton's observations. In other words, the angular unconformity was dramatic evidence that the earth is far more than four times as old as Hadrian's Wall. Hutton could not have known how long development of an angular unconformity requires, but we now know that the one near Jedburgh developed over a period of seventy million years, or seven hundred *thousand* centuries. And even that is less than two percent of the total age of our planet. Ussher's timetable was a million times too short.

Hutton concluded that Earth's age must be far greater than Ussher had claimed, though just how old could not be determined during his lifetime. The actual time scale became knowable only in modern times, principally through the use of radiometric dating, as described in Appendix A. But the simple observation that our planet is more than a few thousand years old was violently at odds with the received timetable. The precision – better than one part per million – and the biblical infallibility of Ussher's calendar were in unavoidable conflict with the geologic data: sixty centuries are not remotely sufficient for the processes whose results are so clearly visible.

James Hutton was right, but he was ahead of his time. On the basis of no lesser authority than the revealed word of God, Hutton was viciously attacked by contemporaries who rejected ideas of rock formation and motion that would have stretched God's busy week's work, as we now know, over billions of years. And Hutton's chronology was soon found to possess another evil aspect: it provided plenty of time for slow Darwinian development of species. You can't have Darwin without Hutton: Ussher's chronology doesn't provide enough time for evolution to play out. To this day the irreconcilability of Darwin and Hutton with Ussher is a major sticking point with religious fundamentalists, causing them to insist on pathetic nonsense like "creation science." More generally, if the Bible is to be understood as a historical record, then the conclusions of Hutton, Darwin, Galileo, Kepler, and Copernicus are impossible. So the issue is joined and the ancient allies, science and religion, are incompatible...it would seem.

CHAPTER 3:
The Author of Geology

Can that be true? Are the ancient allies, science and religion, incompatible? Of course not. We can benefit from both routes to understanding.

We do need to recognize the disconnect between the young-earth calendar of Bishop Ussher and the chronology of modern geology, which confidently asserts that Earth is very old. One can hold in one's hand rocks that cooled almost four billion years ago when our planet was comparatively young: a mere six hundred million years old. The oldest known rock is the result of partial melting of still older rock but there is a limit: the planet coalesced just a little over four and a half billion years ago, so no native rock older than that will be found here, though it's possible that a comet could have deposited rock somewhat older. The universe is much older than our planet. As I said above, cosmologists calculate the age of the universe at a little under fourteen billion years; this figure changes a bit now and again as new data and analyses come to light, but a range of a few billion years seems to include the true age with high confidence.

But the differing timetables don't have to concern us too much. The creation myths in Genesis actually show interesting similarities to the events described by scientists. Creation is described as a process, beginning with a void and successively adding more and more order, and culminating in humankind. Like Genesis, the leading cosmological hypothesis describes creation of the universe in a single instant (though this idea presents great difficulties and will probably need to be modified.) The initially formless Earth of Genesis is geologically sound: our planet cooled from a molten state. The creation of Man after the other animals is described in the first chapter of Genesis, though it is contradicted in the second, which is informed by a different perspective. It is generally accepted by those who accept the evidence for evolution – humans evolved from other animals, so the others must have been here before us – and also by believers in a literal Eden. Genesis represented the best thinking of its time.

Genesis, Hutton, and Darwin

The theology of Genesis and the scientific advances of Hutton, Darwin, and the rest all demonstrate important truths for us. In attempting to reconstruct events in some detail, myth must be distinguished from prehistory. Though both are valuable, each is valuable in its own way. We know things now that were unavailable to the ancients. We don't have to choose between science and religion, as there is no incompatibility at the core, but we do have to choose between the chronology of modern geology and that of Bishop Ussher, between Darwin and a literal Eden with its infestation of talking serpents, between Copernicus and Western medieval cosmology. Many choose geology, Darwin, and Copernicus, and then go on to infer absence of a divine power from rejection of the historical accuracy of Genesis. Others deny the clear evidence of their God-given senses because they imagine that it contradicts God's revelation.

Both groups are too hasty. It is a primitive error of logic to reason from rejection of the historical accuracy of Genesis to a conclusion that there cannot be a divine power. All that can be concluded is that there cannot be a divine power whose history is accurately described in Genesis. The discovery that the universe is a million times as old as Bishop Ussher reckoned doesn't eliminate the possibility that some creative energy is acting; it only changes the time over which this energy acts. Science is the best approach we have for discovering hard facts about the material universe. Faith concerns our response to God's bounty and mercy. Properly understood, the two approaches reinforce each other. They are incompatible only if one confuses the deep metaphorical truths of the Bible with the kind of data in which science specializes.

The creator of the universe transcends any myth his creatures can create about him. It is not true that God pulled Eve from Adam's chest six thousand years ago. It *is* true, and no less amazing, that four billion years after the solid Earth came into existence Mozart was pulled from its stones and composed *Don Giovanni.* The process took millions of centuries: Mozart was not created in a day nor Earth in six. But the apparent chaos described by cosmological theories led, billions of years later, to at least one verdant planet capable of supporting life and of housing creators of great art and music.

We understand in part the DNA code that has been evolving for billions of years, but the fact that we can understand it does not imply that the code must have come into existence spontaneously. A Cryptographer's hand is not provable but may reasonably be suspected. The fact that geology is slow proves only that God is patient: the author of geology has been active for a long time, as Hutton surmised. It is not inherently more absurd to suppose that all of this order resulted from purposeful creation than to suppose that it came about by chance, against staggering odds. There is controversy over the authorship of the Shakespearian canon, but we are pretty sure that these plays were in fact *not* composed by a roomful of monkeys typing at random.

At one time God's existence was considered proved – even rendered self-evident – by our own presence as sentient beings. Like all such proofs, this proof turned out to be inadequate. Darwin demonstrated that we could have evolved from earlier forms, Hutton showed that there was plenty of time, and subsequent evidence makes it clear that we did. The demolition of the supposed proof seemed to some to imply God's *non*existence. But it was not God that was demolished – only the "proof." Nothing in Darwin's discovery rules out the existence of a creative energy, and Darwin never wrote that he had eliminated the possibility of God, though in old age he did become a skeptic.

God's existence is neither proved nor disproved; it is a matter of faith. It is surely plausible, though never provable, that whatever is responsible for the existence of everything we experience is a willfully creative energy. A livable planet from an unimaginable dense hot plasma; the composer of *Don Giovanni* from the molten core and solid stone of Earth; and from primitive chains of amino acids, individuals who can wonder about God: it is not preposterous that changes like these fit a creative plan. And certainly there is nothing in the insights of science that is incompatible with a role for God. Rather, the more we learn about physical laws, the more we are drawn to believe that these are the laws of God. Like the Chacoans, we can sense the mutual witness of science and spirituality, each testifying to the value of their fusion.

A Creator's Love

So, in the permanent absence of proof, we accept that there may be a plan, name the planner God, and try to understand something about him. God is wholly different from us and in fundamental terms we cannot know him. A timeless entity who is the author and ground of being and who could set in motion the fabric of space-time seems to have few points of correspondence with the children of Earth. This points to his transcendence: his extent in all ways beyond our ken. Tillich wrote that we can make only symbolic statements about God. But if we have to resort to metaphor to express what is humanly inexpressible, these metaphors provide a means to relate to the Creator. I would suggest that the relationship itself may be all that we are equipped to know. The relationship relies on God's immanence: his *choice* to be present for us here.

The Sunday school metaphor, "God is love", is an interesting prototype. "God is love" is an affirmation about the relationship we feel with the creator. But there is a basis for our feeling. We do know that God's creation contains a home for us. We can breathe the air and eat the vegetables. The temperature does not freeze us, nor do we spontaneously catch fire. Scientific knowledge points out to us any number of examples of simple amenities that make life possible.

Water is a humble but important case. It is central to our existence because life started in the sea and because most of our body weight is water. Water is so common that we don't think much about it except when it is scarce, but it has remarkable properties. Every child learns in school that substances expand upon heating and contract – become denser – upon cooling. But water is an exception. As it is cooled it reaches its densest point at a temperature of 4° Celsius, or 39° Fahrenheit. If it is cooled below this temperature it stops contracting and begins to expand. This phenomenon – a substance that expands when cooled – was mysterious for a long time, but we now understand that the expansion results from water's unique structure. Upon cooling, water forms clusters of molecules that have a slightly more open – less dense – configuration. The opening of the structure continues as water is frozen, so ice at the freezing point is less dense than liquid water at the same temperature.

If you're wondering why you should care about this obscure fact, consider its consequence: the decrease in density allows ice to float on water. Icebergs don't sink but instead cruise majestically on the surface of polar oceans. For almost all other materials the solid form is more dense than the liquid and sinks to the bottom. The crucial effect of the unique structure of water is that when a lake or sea becomes icy the ice remains on top of the water. In this position it is subject to changes in the weather, so ice comes and goes with the seasons. People can play hockey in Winter without getting their feet wet; the ice melts in Summer and they can dive without bumping their heads. If ice sank to the bottom it would last through the summer and accumulate over the years. In addition to disappointing prospective hockey players, removal of this much liquid water from the ecosystem would be an ecological disaster. If water were like almost all other substances, ice would sink and Earth might be uninhabitable. Instead the deck is stacked in favor of our survival.

The fact that ice floats has been known for ages. The importance of this fact for human survival has also been known for a long time. Now that we know how this is accomplished, it's possible to feel disappointed, if not cheated. One might say, "Floating ice was a miracle, God's grace allowing life on our planet. Now it's been reduced to some boring rigmarole about open structures or whatever." That's the attitude of people who want God to be a stage magician, who want miracle and mystery, in Dostoyevsky's term. The stage magician never reveals his methods, but we don't need to insist on mystery to explain things we now understand.

The deck is stacked in favor of our survival by normal processes obeying normal physical laws. It is true that conditions here favor our survival because we have adapted to them. But if conditions included temperatures so high that all elements would exist as gasses, or so low that virtually everything would be solid, I don't see how evolution of intelligent beings could occur. Intelligence arises in coherent living creatures; gasses would disperse before life developed, and solids do not support the complex internal chemistry life requires. The processes of life are possible only in a very narrow temperature range. We are adapted to the conditions here, but there are probably few sets of conditions to which any form of intelligent life could adapt. At least one of those sets of conditions exists in at least one planet in God's universe, and we make our home here. One could say that we are welcome. A creator expresses his love in this way.

Understanding Amazing Things

Tillich tells us that God is our ground of being: in effect, he is being itself. Saint Paul says something similar: "In him we live and move and have our being…"[27] The universe and everything in it was created by God; we have spoken of God as the creative energy that calls forth the universe. But God does not require the universe to exist in order to exist himself. For *anything* to come into being, God is the basis, the requirement, the originator, the ground.

Our universe came into being about fourteen billion years ago and has a radius approaching fourteen billion light years or somewhat less than a hundred billion trillion miles. That's pretty old and pretty big by our standards, but not *infinitely* big or old. The universe is not a trillion years old or a quadrillion trillion miles across, and if it were it would still not be infinite. While creating such a thing is an enormous feat, it is limited: finite. But God is not only the creator of our universe, not only the creator of life, not only the creator

27 Acts 17:28

of humanity. He is the basis of being itself. This conveys a status of an entirely different order, with no limitation. We don't refer to a hundred billion trillion mile God, or a fourteen billion year God, but *God*, unique, incomparable, not a larger or more powerful version of ourselves but the ground of being. That's what we mean by a monotheistic God rather than one of many capricious, powerful spirits. This understanding makes monotheism self-evident: there are many beings but only one *being*. So the statement that God is our ground of being seems to imply monotheism.

It appears that spiritual yearnings began with an attempt to understand phenomena that were otherwise incomprehensible to primitive people. It is a human trait, to a degree unknown in other animals, to organize our experience in terms of general rules. (Interestingly, this also seems to be the beginning of science; we see again that these paths to understanding are closely related.) So miracles – events and phenomena that were mysterious, numinous, explicable only as divine displays of power – were probably the original stimulus for thinking about God. It was a fusion of what we now call science and religion, and this approach to God was serviceable for many thousands of years.

The trouble was that eventually the mystery became the message, at least as institutional religion saw things. The quest for understanding hit a fork in the road. The faithful were encouraged to contemplate the awful superiority of a deity who could do unimaginable things. The faithful were emphatically *not* encouraged to try to understand these events and phenomena in terms of accessible natural law. The mystery was diminished, along with the power of the Church, to the extent that people understood the process. There is precedent for this concern on the part of the religious authorities. It seems likely that shamans built their power, even in the earliest days, by cloaking their efforts in mystery; the pattern is seen in primitive tribes today.

But since the time of Darwin, natural understandings of amazing things have proliferated and have evoked a reaction from the Church, which has tended to place religion in opposition to facts we learn from other sources. In a technically advanced age we need a more sophisticated understanding, one that emphasizes the consistency of spiritual truth with all other truth. Virtually everything about God is mysterious to us, but there is no need to argue for God's power by making mysteries or miracles out of things we are capable of understanding.

Miracles and Other Wonders

The Latin root for the word miracle is *mirus*: wonder. *Mirabile dictu* means "wonderful to tell." The word "miracle" can be understood in more than one sense, but the most common sense of the word is magic: an apparent fracture of the laws of nature. The Old Testament is full of displays of God's power. Joshua commands the sun to stop moving through the sky and the sun obeys. Sticks are turned into snakes.[28] Seas are rolled back so that God's favorites can pass with dry feet.[29] The Old Testament writers were not thinking in terms of natural law; they saw miracles as revelations of God's will. Less spectacular but still impressive power displays are reported frequently today: a plaster saint weeps, a vial of dried blood turns liquid on a feast day, a shroud displays an image of Jesus. They are regarded as clear signs of God's presence, tangible evidence that eliminates the need to think or meditate. God's miraculous intervention is seen as a comforting reassurance that God is active in our environment. But there's no need for this reassurance. God's real deeds of power – creation of the universe, development of humanity, the incarnation of meaning in a man – are far more potent demonstration. People criticize religion as primitive superstition that has outlived its usefulness, and they're right – *if* we see God only as the magician who reaches into our world and does inexplicable things. We do not worship the god of weeping plaster saints. This is not how his immanence is expressed.

The New Testament also contains accounts of amazing events. But most of the New Testament is not history, any more than most of the Old Testament is. The New Testament is primarily a collection

---

28 Exodus 7:10

29 Exodus 14:21-22

of spiritual documents. There is no need to focus on whether Jesus actually multiplied food to feed thousands of listeners.[30] Perhaps before he told the disciples, "*You* give them something to eat," he simply touched people's hearts so that they shared the ample food they had quietly brought to the meeting. That change in attitude would be a more profound miracle than a magical multiplication of bread and fish portions, and more central to Jesus's mission. All of the New Testament miracle stories are concerned with spiritual issues. The calming of the seas[31] and walking on water[32] suggest that God is always with us and we have nothing to fear. The therapeutic miracles point to a healing relationship that transcends disease. The raising of Lazarus[33] portends raising of humanity to the New Being. If their sole point were a demonstration of power they would only be parlor tricks, no more impressive than similar stunts reported as performed by other figures.

If the biblical understanding of miracles did not focus on suspension of natural law, some of our contemporaries do have that focus. Yet miracles understood as occasions when God suspends the rules happen only in some other time or some other place. If we modify the sense of the word to include wonders, without requiring that they be supernatural, we are awash in miracles. Suppose a writer of fantasy a mere hundred years ago sent a time traveler to our present. The traveler might report back to his own time, "They talk to each other effortlessly from North America to Japan. A box of light shows pictures of things happening on the other side of the globe. They can send messages instantly, or find the answer to any question, just by tapping a few keys..." One of the late science fiction writer Arthur C. Clarke's rules of prediction is, "Any sufficiently advanced technology is indistinguishable from magic." Our traveler, though from a time within living memory today, would lack the technology to understand

---

30 Mark 6:35-44

31 Matthew 8:23-26

32 Matthew 14:25-31

33 John 11:1-44

telephones, or television, or the Internet. He would see these things as miracles, and he would be right to recognize wonders. But we know that our wonders do not break the laws of physics, and we recognize that the technical wonders of the next generation, if we could see them today, would be incomprehensible to us as other than miraculous.

To pick just one example, much of what happens in a hospital today would astound a doctor of a generation or two ago. Organs are transplanted from other individuals, or replaced by mechanical devices even to the point of an artificial heart. Drugs cure the causes of most of the deaths of a few years ago; we have had to find new things to die of. It is common to speak of medical miracles and miracle drugs. This figure of speech is in fact literally correct. These wonders come from God, working through the hands and brains of his most advanced creation: human beings. But of course they are not supernatural.

The Shmoo

In this sense, we are surrounded by miracles that we have ceased to notice after millennia of familiarity. Sometimes such miracles are emphasized in unfamiliar ways. Al Capp's comic strip, *Li'l Abner*, featured a strange and magical creature called the Shmoo in an extended sequence that began in 1948. Shaped like a furry bowling pin, the Shmoo could supply anything people wanted. Without charge it gave white or chocolate milk. It was delighted to be broiled, when it tasted like steak, or fried, in which case it tasted like chicken. Yet it was as nutritious as green vegetables. And it could provide affection: it made a mellifluous sound when hugged. It multiplied as needed, lived on air, and was freely available to everyone.

Needless to say, it was seen by sinister interests to be a threat to the economic order, and was promptly exterminated.[34] Abner's

---

34 Although in the 1960's he became an outspoken conservative foe of student activists, Capp's views were much more liberal during the Truman administration. Nevertheless the Shmoo caused Capp to be attacked by Socialists for unseemly levity or something.

girlfriend, Daisy Mae, was heartbroken, but Abner consoled her by pointing out that the Shmoo is still with us. The Earth, powered by the sun, provides everything the Shmoo supplied and more: "Shmoos *hain't* make believe. The hull earth is one!!" The value of the Shmoo was that it enabled us to see as miraculous something that had become commonplace. "Blessed art Thou, O Lord," Jews pray, recognizing a miracle when they see one, *"who brings out bread from the ground."*

It is common to say, "The Lord will provide." In fact, the Lord *has* provided. We know that telephones, television, computers, organ transplants, and new drugs and devices are based on technology, not magic. The absence of magic can also be established, though it is less widely recognized, in ancient wonders that have been around far longer than the human race. It appears magical – it certainly is wonderful – that crops grow and provide food, but in fact all of the chemistry involved in creating bread out of dirt and sunshine is understandable, and will eventually be *fully* understood, in natural terms. We understand quite a lot of it today. Living entities capable of becoming human beings are created after fertilization in Petri dishes, and we are on the verge of still more profound manipulations for which our science is ready, though our culture and philosophy probably are not.

None of this violates natural law, or requires specific activity of the hand of God on a day-to-day basis. All of it is miraculous: wonderful. We are not fed by magical intervention but by ordinary miraculous chemistry. The laws of nature are God's laws. He has no need to suspend them; they provide for whatever he needs to get done in the universe. For the heaviest lifting, he has natural phenomena like gravitation, nuclear forces, electricity, magnetism, and probably some others we don't know about yet. For acts of intelligent kindness he has our hands, our brains, and our hearts.

Natural Law's Creator

While there is much more that is so far unknown than is known, we are learning to understand the processes of nature more and more deeply. We will understand them completely, in the sense that we can describe them and can reproduce them in the laboratory. That's what the word "understand" means to a scientist. It does not mean that we comprehend the mind of the creator, his purposes, his motivations, the love that lies behind what he has given us. Science is no use to us there. But while the processes of life are mysterious and wonderful, they are not miracles in the supernatural sense.

The sun, for example, is a reasonably well understood thermonuclear reaction vessel: something like a gigantic hydrogen bomb. It is benign because we need its heat and light and because it is ninety-three million miles away. We think we know how it assumed its present form and how it produces heat and light. We definitely know, unfortunately, how to build a hydrogen bomb closer to home, and nothing supernatural is required. We have to find a way to live with the dangerous consequences of this knowledge.

The discovery that the most awesome physical phenomena we experience can be couched in terms of prosaic principles is profoundly disturbing to some people who hold tightly to traditional religious ideas. That's why we have people – even a few with scientific degrees and university chairs – who write learned tomes on intelligent design or found museums of "creation science." But the discovery that prosaic physical principles underlie the development of the universe, and even life itself, should not be unsettling. Nothing in the physicist's explanation of things vitiates the role of God. From the theist's perspective God is the author of the laws of physics and of all natural law.

The creator God created a rational universe. By the way, this does not mean that God isn't currently active in the universe; the perspective of the Deists is not being proposed. God is active today, but he acts within the bounds of the natural laws he created and through the medium of human beings coached by the Holy Spirit. There is no proof that he never acts in any other way, but I know of no convincing evidence that he ever does.

We now recognize that the story of events in the Garden of Eden six thousand years ago is a myth, valuable and instructive but never intended to be taken literally. But we also have some understanding of the factual early history of the universe. The outline of events since the beginning of time is becoming fairly clear. This knowledge does not in any way imply the absence of God, though it does demolish the idea that the universe has existed for only a few dozen centuries. Of course our detailed knowledge contains many gaps and what we think we know is, like all scientific knowledge, tentative and subject to correction. But despite the gaps, no magic needs to be invoked. On the basis of what we know now we can say, "God created the world and here's some information about how he did it."

The Beginning

We begin at the beginning: the instant when the universe came into being. (We have no reliable information about how *that* was accomplished, though interesting speculations have been proposed, some of which have been described by Joseph Silk.[35]) Most cosmologists accept the Big Bang hypothesis, which holds that the universe began suddenly fourteen billion years ago. We may call that first instant t_0, pronounced "tee zero." The physicists' term of art for whatever the situation was at t_0 is "initial conditions." We cannot speak of times before t_0 because time, like space, could not exist without the existence of the universe. And we cannot discuss the physics of t_0 itself, except to say that it is beyond our ken. Whatever already existed at the instant of creation is outside science as we know it – at least so far. Science concerns itself with subsequent events: how the initial conditions led to the current situation.

One form of the Big Bang hypothesis conceives the universe as initially occupying only a single point of zero size. This leads to mathematical and other scientific problems, including infinitely high temperature and infinitely high density at t_0, so we conclude that it is not true. The initial existence of the universe as a single point follows directly from the General Theory of Relativity, which is why we expect that general relativity will need to be modified. One approach under consideration is known as string theory, though it

35 Silk, Joseph, *The Big Bang*, Third Edition, New York, W.H. Freeman and Company, 2001

may be premature to call it a theory, because it has little contact with observation so far. The string picture says the fundamental components of the universe are not particles, but tiny strings.[36] In this system, the universe at its creation, while unimaginably small, would be larger than a single point.

Another alternative to the Big Bang has been proposed by Stephen Hawking, the world's best-known cosmologist. Hawking was invited to the Vatican in 1981 for a conference on cosmology.[37] The Vatican conference communicated the Church's approval of the Big Bang: this hypothesis is consistent with the first verse of Genesis and thus with Church doctrine. In receiving the Vatican's approval, Hawking decided not to mention the fact that he had recently begun to favor a different hypothesis. The new hypothesis eliminates the creation of the universe at a single instant, though mathematically there is still a t_0. Instead of the universe being created at t_0 it simply occupies a given span in space and time. If we count three dimensions of space – say length, width, and height – and one of time, that's a total of four dimensions to describe where something is in space-time. According to Hawking's hypothesis the universe is a four-dimensional egg whose extent in time starts with t_0. The egg hypothesis solves some mathematical inconveniences associated with the Big Bang because it does not postulate that the universe was a single point at t_0. Roughly speaking, we can say that in this picture the universe doesn't have any sharp points like the point at t_0 in the Big Bang hypothesis. But since it doesn't identify an instant of creation analogous to the one in Genesis, it doesn't so clearly ingratiate itself with Church doctrine. So Hawking kept tactfully silent about the egg hypothesis when he spoke at the Vatican.

Because it eliminates a creation event, the egg hypothesis (Hawking calls it "the no boundary" hypothesis, for sound

36 See, for example, Greene, Brian, *The Elegant Universe*, New York and London, W. W. Norton & Company, 1999

37 Hawking, Steven W, *A Brief History of Time*, Toronto and New York, Bantam Books, 1988

mathematical reasons that we will not go into) has been interpreted by some to leave no room for God to act. But this interpretation is based on a misunderstanding of theistic thinking. The Big Bang hypothesis also holds that there is no space outside the universe and no time before t_0. (There may or may not be an end to the universe in the future; if so time ends when the universe ends.) The answer to the famous question of what God was doing in the depths of time before he created the universe has a clear answer: the Big Bang hypothesis and the no boundary hypothesis agree with Genesis that there *was* no time before t_0. As Genesis puts it, t_0 was "the beginning."

The universe is fourteen billion years old and God was already present at its beginning, but God is not a trillion or a quadrillion years old because fourteen billion years is all the time there has ever been. God is not old, he is eternal. The creative energy behind the universe is not confined in time or space, as these metrics exist only for our universe. God is no more cramped by the egg hypothesis than by the Big Bang. God is eternally creative and creation is continuous. Hawking's egg hypothesis, like the Big Bang and all scientific cosmological hypotheses, is silent on the question of who lays the egg.

Being and Its Ground

Scientists generally accept that there was a t_0. More fundamentally, most people will acknowledge that there is a universe. On reflection, this is an extraordinary fact, and one that is extraordinarily important to us. But creation is not a function of the universe. At a still more fundamental level, there is *being*. Being is almost a primitive concept. The dictionary definition starts with "the quality or state of having existence." [38] Existence is defined as "reality as opposed to appearance…reality as presented in experience." Both definitions go on and on from their starting points, and neither really tells us anything we didn't feel we knew before. Let's assume we know what being is, even if we have trouble defining it. There is no rational explanation

---

38 Merriam-Webster's Collegiate Dictionary,
© 1994 Merriam-Webster, Inc.

for being, but only the most hard core philosopher will deny that we have it. For the rest of us it is a basic fact. Being is everywhere; we can't get away from it.

This is true even in situations where we might suppose there is nothing. Physicists spend a lot of time working with vacuum. Many physical experiments are performed in chambers from which almost all of the air – all but one part in a trillion, or less – has been pumped. One might think that what is inside such a chamber is approaching a state of nothingness – a state of non-being – but it is not. We can go beyond actual experiments with vacuum to imagine a chamber from which *all* molecules have been pumped. What is inside this hypothetical chamber – which in real experiments can only be approached, never reached – is perfect vacuum. But this idealized condition isn't a state of non-being. Even in perfect vacuum there is still time and space. Measurements in centimeters and seconds can be made and have their usual meanings. Gravity is active and there is probably light and certainly infrared radiation, unless the temperature of the walls of the chamber is absolute zero. Further, a strange phenomenon called vacuum fluctuations was discovered in the twentieth century. It is related to Heisenberg's principle, discussed in Chapter 12. Vacuum fluctuations means that even if there doesn't seem to be anything present, all kinds of particles of matter and quanta of energy appear fleetingly and disappear spontaneously all the time in vacuum. So a perfect vacuum is by no means empty. There is being even in vacuum. Language has a hard time expressing the situation, but we have to say (sorry, grammarians) that a perfect vacuum is not nothing.

We can go further. Being is not only everywhere, it is every*when*. The universe is about fourteen billion years old. While we cannot speak of time before the universe, we can speak of a state in which the universe does not exist. But this is not a state of nothingness; there is still being, since God exists. Being does not depend on the existence of the universe; being is more fundamental than the universe. At t_0 there was already being and always had been. But in the absence of a creative energy I see no reason to expect that there would have been being. *Nothing* seems like the situation that would exist in the absence of a basis for being.[39] But we don't have nothing. We have being, and that is by no means a trivial observation. It's tempting to say that the creative energy (i.e., God) creates being, but that can't be right because if the creative energy exists there is already being. The creative energy is coeternal with being, which is close to being a restatement of Tillich's teaching that God is our ground of being.

The timeless creative principle that breathes being: we name that principle God. God, in Tillich's term, is the ground of being. The existence of such a principle cannot be proved from the fact that the universe exists any more than it is disproved by scientific advances. But it is plausible. Those who state, "I have no need for that hypothesis" have no alternative hypothesis to account for the fact of being. Being would be a ridiculous hypothesis except that we are continuously immersed in it. The insights of physics, chemistry, biology, and geology have been cited as reasons to believe there is no god, as replacements for the primitive association of a god with every important environmental challenge. But scientific insights do not argue for atheism. Almost everyone agrees that there is being. This suggests the need for a ground of being.

Now we see the insights of science and faith converging: we see that the author of geology is the ground of being.

---

39 This raises a semantic problem. Actually one shouldn't talk about *nothing* as a situation, as that seems to make it *something*. Since we don't have language to discuss this issue consistently, we'll just plod along and ignore the problem.

CHAPTER 4:
The New Teleology

At this rate, we'll be here until the end of time…if it has one. Our sketch of very ancient history has stalled at the first instant. We'll have to make some progress to add further support to the claim that spiritual and scientific understandings of the physical universe are complementary. To bring our sketch forward, we recall that the Big Bang hypothesis and Hawking's no boundary hypothesis agree that at t_0 the universe was very small: if it wasn't a single mathematical point, perhaps it was the size of the point of a needle, or maybe a trillion trillion trillion trillion times smaller than that. It was packed with matter and energy. By matter we mean, in every day terms, *stuff*: tangible objects, solid, liquid, or gas, or peculiar types of matter we won't get into here. By energy we mean the ability to make things happen: the kinetic energy of a swinging baseball bat that can knock a ball out of the park, or the potential energy of masses of water at the top of Niagara Falls. When the water falls it gains speed going down and some of its potential energy is converted to kinetic energy. But the total energy, kinetic plus potential, remains the same.

For some purposes it's hard to specify the difference between matter and energy. In fact Albert Einstein deduced, early in the last century, that they are equivalent. Matter can be converted into energy and vice versa. This is the only way the total energy can change; the total of mass and energy combined never changes.

The equivalence of matter and energy is the basis of Einstein's famous equation, $E = mc^2$, which tells us how much energy E is equivalent to a mass m. Mass is a measure of how much matter is present. When you convert a given mass into energy, you get a *lot* of energy, and Einstein's equation tells just how much. The quantity c is the speed of light. Since light travels very fast, c is a large number, and c^2 (c squared, or c times c) is a huge number. Consequently, a little mass is converted into a huge amount of energy, as the residents of Hiroshima tragically learned in 1945. Only a single ounce of matter was converted to release the energy that leveled their city.[40] Evidence even before 1945 had already confirmed Einstein's theory, so in certain situations we speak of mass-energy rather than independently of mass and energy.

Mass-energy is neither created nor destroyed. All the mass-energy there is was present at t_0, according to the Big Bang picture and others. Through all of time the amount of mass-energy in the universe has remained constant. Small as it was, the universe at t_0 was dense with all the mass-energy it holds today. It was thus an unimaginably chaotic environment. Nothing we would recognize as ordinary matter could have existed there.

The Expanding Universe

The past fourteen billion years have been eventful, as the universe evolved according to the unchanging laws of physics, which are among the laws of God. From the moment of its creation the universe has been expanding. What existed in the time just after t_0 was totally different from matter as we know it today. There was recognizable energy in the form of light, reminding us that God's first reported utterance was "Let there be light!" But it would be billions of years before there was anyone to see the light.

As the universe expanded, the incredible temperatures and pressures of the initial state were reduced. Within a fraction of a second, normal protons and electrons emerged. At lower temperatures, perhaps three hundred thousand years later, a proton could capture an electron to produce the first atom, hydrogen. Other atoms followed, beginning with helium, so now the universe contains a great deal of ordinary matter, and chemistry can play its life-producing role.

---

40 Hawking, Steven and Mlodinow, Leonard,
A Briefer History of Time, New York, Bantam Dell, 2005

Without any violation of natural law life has come into existence, humanity has developed, culture has evolved, and Don Giovanni has been composed.

The needlepoint-sized universe expanded to its current enormous size and it's still expanding. The mass-energy in the universe is now spread over a volume of billions upon billions of cubic light years, diluting it so that most space in the universe is nearly empty of matter as we know it. According to Silk,[41] the mean density of matter in the universe is around one particle per cubic meter. That's better vacuum than can be achieved in any physics laboratory.

Yet there are places that are densely filled because matter is not evenly distributed: under the influence of gravity quite a lot of it has aggregated, or clumped, into galaxies and stars. The process, as currently understood, is described in some detail by Silk. A galaxy is a huge collection of stars but galaxies actually come into existence before most stars: matter aggregates into galaxies and then much of the matter in each galaxy aggregates into stars and sometimes planets. From the viewpoint of people living on a planet (Earth) orbiting a star (Sol) in a galaxy (the Milky Way), this aggregation could fairly be described as the most important thing that happened for fourteen billion years. Stars and planets are essential to the development of life. We wouldn't be here without aggregation. We could never have evolved in a nearly empty part of the universe.

Stars are essential to us because they are reaction vessels sustaining processes, including thermonuclear reactions, at enormously high pressures and temperatures. Initially the only atomic matter was in the form of light atoms, mainly hydrogen and helium, the two simplest elements. Life requires many additional elements beyond these, and stars are the retorts in which most heavier elements are formed. The processes that produce these heavier elements require the conditions found in the interiors of stars.

While they are formed inside stars, many atoms of these heavy elements are eventually released into the universe at large. A star has a distinct life cycle which frequently comes to a dramatic finale:

41 Silk, Joseph *op. cit.*

billions of years into the life cycle an enormous explosion called a supernova spews out heavy elements from the stellar interior. After the first generation of stars and supernovae, some of the newly available matter, which now included all of the elements rather than just the lightest ones, again aggregated into lumps that became later generation galaxies, suns, and occasionally planets (including ours). So while first generation stars were restricted to light elements, later generation stars included heavy elements. The heavy elements were also incorporated into planets. This ultimately made it possible for life to develop, for we include in our bodies all of the stable elements of Earth.

The Surprising Universe

Since our universe contains living things, it's natural to suppose that life is a normal part of a universe. But that's not the case: the development of intelligent life could not have been reliably predicted. In fact it raises a challenging question: why does our universe support life? Over the past four decades, scientists have taken note of a strange fact: it is difficult – indeed it is very nearly impossible – for a universe to produce living creatures. The arguments are quite technical but there seems little disagreement among experts on this point. Based on what is now known of physics, conditions that permit life to develop in a universe are much more stringent than conditions under which a sterile universe – one that spawns no life – can exist. To put it another way, if you somehow constructed every possible universe, virtually all of them would be sterile. Life is a surprise.

It is particularly noteworthy that this fact was not first noticed by theists trying to make a religious point. It has been observed and confirmed, to their considerable surprise, by some of the top physicists in the world, many of whom were not theists. This is not "creation science." Whether or not it has any implications for theism, it is well accepted in the scientific community.

We can't lay out the scientific details of this discovery, but we can examine a few specimens to get a feeling for how it works. To begin with, the Big Bang and all other viable hypotheses posit a universe that started very small and continues to expand today. We have seen that expansion of the universe was essential to us: we wouldn't be here without it. You might think that the expansion could have been quite slow or quite fast, that any rate within reason would allow the development of life. But it turns out that this is not true. In fact if the rate of expansion one second after t_0 had been smaller by one thousand trillionth (i.e., a quadrillionth) of one percent, Hawking[42] calculates that the expansion would quickly have come to a stop and reversed. Gravitational forces would cause the big bang to be succeeded by a "big crunch" before there was time for life to develop. In other words, the initial expansion was exactly the slowest it could possibly be if life were to develop.

That seems a strange coincidence but what follows is much stranger. The expansion is not only the slowest it could be, but also the fastest it could be if life were to develop. If it had been even one part per million faster the expansion would have been too violent. All the particles of the universe would have rushed away from each other so fast that aggregation could not occur – gravity would not be strong enough ever to pull the particles together – meaning that galaxies, stars, and planets would never have appeared. In that case the elements necessary to life would not have been formed; we have seen that many of these elements are formed within stars. Further, the planetary conditions in which life evolved would not have existed.

The surprising conclusion is that the initial expansion rate could not have been the least bit slower or faster if the universe were not to be sterile. For life to appear in a universe, gravitational forces must exactly balance the initial expansion. That's what happened in our universe. It's as if you flipped a coin expecting it to come down either heads or tails, and it actually landed on edge and stayed there. It's not impossible but it's extremely unlikely.

That makes the density of matter in the first instants after t_0 a

---

42 Hawking, Steven W: *A Brief History of Time*, Toronto and New York, Bantam Books, 1988 quoted in Barbour, Ian G., *When Science Meets Religion*, San Francisco, HarperCollins, 2000

crucially important parameter, and there was one precise value that it had to take if intelligent life were to emerge in the universe. If the initial density had been just slightly greater, resulting in more gravitational attraction pulling the universe together, the expansion would have been slower. If the initial density had been just slightly less the expansion would have been faster. In either case, as we have just seen, the universe would have been sterile.

The expansion rate and the density of matter had to take exact values, or no life could have appeared. Beyond this, the evolution of a universe is governed by a number of physical constants, whose values determine how the universe will develop. Consider for example the ratio of the force constants that determine how strongly particles will attract or repel each other. Forces between electrically charged particles are governed by a relatively strong force constant and can be attractive or repulsive: pulling the particles together or pushing them apart. Up close they determine how matter behaves, but at a distance they cancel each other to a very considerable degree because there are large and nearly equal numbers of positive and negative particles interacting. That is to say a charge will feel an almost equal amount of push and of pull, and will not be much affected overall. Gravitation, on the other hand, is governed by a force constant that is more than a trillion trillion trillion times weaker but is always attractive: there is no repulsive component to the gravitational forces we are familiar with.[43] This means there is no cancellation of attractive and repulsive forces, so over very long distances the pull of gravity becomes dominant.

The relative strengths of the gravitational and electrical force constants are such that we live in a universe where a lot of matter is concentrated by gravitational forces into galaxies, stars, and planets, making living beings possible. If there were a slight change in the ratio of the force constants, the universe would evolve without the appearance of life. This ratio, which apparently could take any value,

43 This statement may someday need to be modified slightly, as there have been suggestions that a weak gravitational push exists. If so, we might have to say that the gravitational force is *mostly* attractive, but the gravitational pull would still dominate over long distances.

in fact must take a single precisely defined value if life is to develop. That is the value it takes in our universe.

Here are two more of the many situations where small changes in the values of constants would make our universe sterile. They're pretty technical so I'll just sketch them. Don't worry if you find them hard to follow. One concerns the ratio of the gravitational force to the force that controls radioactivity: what physicists call the "weak force." The weak force is a lot stronger than the gravitational force but much weaker than the electromagnetic force. If this ratio were slightly different, the elements necessary for life would never be produced. Finally, there's the total amount of mass-energy in the universe. If it were higher the reactions that power stars would proceed too rapidly, and stars would be too hot to sustain life on their planets. If the total mass-energy were smaller stars would not produce the elements needed for life.

Anthropic Principles

There are examples involving many other constants – and probably more that haven't been noticed yet – and ratios between different constants. They all have to fit together with exquisite precision, and we don't know why or how this precision was achieved. There is no known requirement in theory that these constants and ratios take the values they do, but if a single one of the parameters in question had a slightly different value the universe that evolved would be devoid of life. The requirement that all of these parameters take exactly the required values can be pictured by imagining that we toss a large number of coins and require that *every one* of them lands and remains on edge, rather than coming up either heads or tails. You wouldn't bet on such an event unless you had the game rigged somehow. The probability of all this happening by chance is unimaginably small, though it is not zero.

The fact that so many parameters have exactly the required values has raised in some people's minds the old teleologic argument for the existence of God. This was the claim that so intricate a work as man could not have come about without the action of a higher power. The argument was that if one were to take a walk in the woods and come across a finely crafted watch, it would be only reasonable to conclude that there had been a watchmaker. Watches, after all, don't make themselves. So if one finds humans and other intricately constructed animals in the world, there must be a God who crafted them. The teleologic argument was pretty well demolished by the insights of Darwin, in that this proof of God's existence was no longer convincing. Evolution was attacked precisely because it seemed to offer a way for mankind to appear without needing the crafting hand of God. Some people went beyond recognizing that the proof had been rebutted and came to believe that Darwin had rid the universe of God himself. Now scientists have discovered that the game does appear to be rigged: the parameters of the universe are "fine-tuned" in exactly the way they must be for mankind to come into existence. Once again we see an observation being presented as a new proof of the providence of an intelligent and loving God. Instead of God the watchmaker some people postulate God the fine tuner.

To counter the teleologic argument, the anthropic principle has been introduced. Its least controversial form is called the "weak anthropic principle." It states, correctly if not profoundly, that if the conditions for life had *not* existed, there would have been no one to notice this fact. Only a universe where the conditions for life existed could ever produce observers to ponder the question. So only those values of the parameters that make life possible could ever be observed.

Not many people quarrel with the weak anthropic principle – it seems more or less self-evident – but it does not in itself explain fine tuning. It only guarantees that the *absence* of fine tuning could never be observed. So stronger and more controversial forms of the anthropic principle have been proposed. According to the strong anthropic principle, the existence of mankind today somehow causes the constants to take life-producing values fourteen billion years ago! I will not comment further on the stronger statements of the anthropic principle, except to ask whether willingness to swallow such a mechanism demonstrates an unscientifically powerful bias toward keeping God out of the universe.

Does that mean that fine-tuning proves the existence and providence of God? Absolutely not. God's existence is not susceptible to proof and faith has to do with things "not seen." Fine tuning can be explained in at least two ways (and no doubt more) without requiring a higher power.

One candidate explanation notes that coincidences do happen. It may be that the parameters just happen to take the values they need for life to exist. If they didn't, the weak anthropic principle tells us that we wouldn't be around to notice. This would be a long shot for any given universe, but the universe we observe may be one among many in an all-inclusive multiverse. If the multiverse contains enough universes – or perhaps an infinite number of universes – with a sufficient spread in values of the critical constants, there could be at least one universe with the values required for life. If you toss a bunch of coins often enough, sooner or later – much later – they *will* all come down on edge. Again, the weak anthropic principle, which everyone accepts, guarantees that this is the universe we observe. A sterile universe cannot produce observers.

It's not clear where these other universes are. They can't simply be far away: no matter how far you go you're still in this universe with these values of the constants. One can't say the other universes are older or younger than ours, or even that they are contemporaries, because time is defined for us only in this universe. They're not other places or other times; they're just other. It's incomprehensible to us but that doesn't make it impossible.

The multiverse idea can take another form that is easier to envision, in which the universes exist one at a time. Our universe may come to an end in contraction to a very small volume from which a new universe emerges. Perhaps the new universe expands and repeats the whole evolutionary process with different values of the parameters. If this expansion and contraction were repeated enough times – there's no proof that the cycle couldn't be repeated as many times as necessary – a universe might eventually crop up with the fine-tuned values necessary for life. It might take trillions of trillions of years, but there would be no one to become impatient. The weak anthropic principle tells us the universe with the fine-tuned values (or the epoch during which the universe had the fine-tuned values) would be the only one observed.

The multiverse hypothesis in either form appears to me to be untestable. One definition of our universe is that it contains everything that we could ever observe. Another universe in the multiverse is therefore forever hidden from us. And if the other universes exist before the beginning of our time or after the end, we can know nothing about them. So the multiverse hypothesis is no more susceptible to proof – or disproof – than the hypothesis that God set the values of the constants to make life possible. There is no way to decide between these hypotheses, which makes the status of either of them as science quite dubious.

The Possibility of a Deeper Theory

Another way to explain fine tuning is to reexamine our assumptions. Perhaps with deeper understanding of physics we might find some reason that the observed values of the critical constants are the only ones possible. That is, we may have been wrong in assuming that the universe could have developed perfectly well, though without producing life, with other values of the critical parameters. Maybe when we get closer to the final theory we will see that the fine-tuned values of the constants are required for a universe, whether sterile or fecund, to exist. Restrictions like this are discovered frequently.

For now, we can look at a concocted example. Suppose there is a naïve but very smart individual whom we'll call Isaac. Isaac is keenly curious about all the phenomena he notices around him and is a highly skilled experimentalist, but he knows nothing about physics. He observes that objects have effects on each other and decides to study these effects.

The first thing Isaac discovers is that all objects attract each other. By painstaking observation he discovers that there is a force –

he decides to call it "gravity" – between one central object and others in the vicinity. He goes on to find that the attraction grows stronger if the objects are heavier and weaker if they are farther apart. Now Isaac develops a way to make accurate measurements of this force. He finds that the force of gravity one centimeter from the central object is one hundred times as strong as the force ten centimeters from the object. He doesn't need to know anything about physics to discover this, but since the force of gravity is very weak the measurements would be fiendishly difficult to make accurately. Still, he's a clever guy and he manages to get it done.

Next Isaac tries a variety of things to change the force. He rubs the central object briskly with various materials, some of which put an electrical charge on it. (He doesn't know about charge but we do.) Then he does the same thing to the other objects and makes another series of measurements. He discovers that the force between objects is now much stronger. (This time the force may be either a push or a pull, but we're concentrating on how strong the force is.) Isaac decides that rubbing the objects produces an entirely new force, which he decides to call the "electrostatic" force. His measurements tell him that the electrostatic force one centimeter from the central object is exactly one hundred times the force at ten centimeters. This measurement isn't quite so tricky, because electrostatic forces are stronger and thus easier to measure.

Now Isaac defines a parameter – he calls it R – which is the ratio of the decrease in the gravitational force to the decrease in the electrostatic force. He says, "For distances of one centimeter and ten centimeters gravitational force decreases by a factor of one hundred. For those same distances electrostatic force also decreases by a factor of one hundred. One hundred divided by one hundred is one, so for distances of one centimeter and ten centimeters, R is exactly one. How interesting! I will measure the ratio for other distances. Then I will plot these values on a graph to show how R changes with distance."

That's exactly what a scientist would do. Scientists like to plot things and examine relationships, but Isaac is in for a disappointment.

His graphs are not interesting at all, because R is *always* equal to one no matter what distances he uses for his measurements. It never varies. Isaac thinks he has found a mysterious example of fine-tuning, because he has no way of explaining why R is restricted to a single value. But he's wrong: with our superior knowledge of physics we can say that the invariance of R is not an example of fine-tuning. We know how to calculate R from more basic principles and we can show that it is restricted to the value one.[44]

The Habitable Universe

So much for the concocted example. My point is that there may be some deep theory guaranteeing that the critical constants of the universe are restricted to the fine-tuned values permitting the development of life. Maybe there's "some boring rigmarole" that's beyond our present understanding. We observe that the values are fine-tuned but don't know why. For the present it looks like magic. Like Isaac, we don't know enough physics today to see how fine-tuning is guaranteed, but some day in the future that may no longer be true.

It is a fact, confirmed by scientists of all theological persuasions or none, that numerous constants have exactly the values necessary to make life possible in our universe. This certainly does not prove the existence of a benevolent God, since there are other possible explanations. We've considered two candidates, the multiverse hypothesis and the possibility that deeper knowledge of physics restricts the constants to the fine-tuned values. Either might explain the observed result and surely there are other possibilities. But theists may consider the following passage from Isaiah to be relevant:

For thus says the Lord, who created the heavens (he is God!), who formed the

---

44 The details don't matter for our purposes, but it turns out that the surface area of a sphere increases with the square of the sphere's diameter, and this fact guarantees that R must be exactly one for long range effects like electrostatic and gravitational forces.

*earth and made it (he established it; he did not create a chaos, **he formed it to be inhabited!**): I am the Lord, and there is no other.*[45] (Emphasis added.)

Though there's no proof, it's reasonable for theists to suspect that God formed the universe to be our home.

A majority of the people involved in developing the scientific information we have sketched probably would deny that there is a god. They focus on their scientific work, not on any fusion with spiritual issues. But nothing prevents those of us who are theists from seeing the scientific fact of fine tuning as God's earliest greeting to his people: "I've left the light on for you."

---

45 Isaiah 45:18

SECTION 2:
The Meaning of Being

We believe in one Lord, Jesus Christ, the only Son of God, eternally begotten of the Father, God from God, Light from Light, true God from true God, begotten, not made, of one Being with the Father. Through him all things were made. For us and for our salvation he came down from heaven: by the power of the Holy Spirit he became incarnate from the Virgin Mary, and was made man. For our sake he was crucified under Pontius Pilate; he suffered death and was buried. On the third day he rose again in accordance with the Scriptures; he ascended into heaven and is seated at the right hand of the Father. He will come again in glory to judge the living and the dead, and his kingdom will have no end.

CHAPTER 5:
The Chemistry of Life

God is the ground of being. He is the creator of the universe and its contents, including human beings. We are coming to understand the physical universe fairly well, though there's a lot more work to do. Relevant scientific advances are constantly being made, but they do not suggest the absence of a role for God. Yet even if we believe that God has left the light on for us we have as yet not considered why he would do that. That's the question I asked Professor Tillich half a century ago. The physical universe that we see does not in itself proclaim its meaning. Our partial understanding of how the universe got to be the way it is tells us nothing about its significance, or whether it has any. And the meaning of being is an even deeper question than the meaning of the universe.

To discover what that meaning might be we have to look further. We have sketched the massive physical forces that cause matter to condense into stars and planets, making life possible. But if the meaning is to be comprehensible and relevant to us it should include some explicit reference to living things, and eventually to humanity. So in this chapter we'll talk about life and we'll talk about chemistry. Life as we experience it is a lot more than chemistry. We equate it with spirit, with consciousness. It is what makes you and me totally different beings from a couple of rocks. Art, music, dance, literature fill us with life, make us appreciate life. If a drink is fizzy and peps me up, it seems lively. Life is what we find in lively things.

A tornado is lively, even if it destroys living things. But a tornado does not have life in the sense that you and I have life, or even in the sense that a mosquito has life. There is a physical basis to life, one that comes long before humanity or spirituality or culture. Human culture has existed for only one thousandth of one percent of the time there has been life on Earth. We'll get to humanity one step at a time. Our next step is to discuss the processes of life, which are governed by chemistry.

That's a provocative statement in itself, and in fact we're going to talk about life in ways that some will find offensive. For a biologist life has a very specific meaning. It is the characteristic that is present in entities that can reproduce themselves. A group of molecules that can make another similar group has life. That's the first step; you have to get that far before you can begin to add spirit to life. And while we are far from understanding everything, life in this narrow sense is not fundamentally mysterious. We'll talk about life as understood by chemistry, beginning with a forward jump to a time nine billion years after t_0.

Moving Rocks

With the constants of the universe fine-tuned for success, Earth came into distinct existence about four and a half billion years ago, as an agglomeration of the materials at hand. Near the surface were light elements, prominently including silicon, oxygen, hydrogen, nitrogen, and carbon, among others. We surface dwellers encounter these elements all the time, primarily in compounds. Rocks contain silicon and oxygen; water is a compound of hydrogen and oxygen; air is mostly nitrogen but contains significant carbon and a great deal of oxygen, and so forth.

Heavier elements settled farther below the surface. After a reactor like the ones that failed in Japan in 2011 is turned off, the radioactive fuel rods continue to generate dangerous levels of heat. If cooling is removed the rods can easily get hot enough to melt themselves and other parts of the reactor. Similarly, some of the heavy elements deep in our planet are radioactive, generating huge amounts of energy. Earth was initially liquid, but cooled about four billion years ago to the point where rock at the surface was solid. The deeper layers are much hotter, as Hutton surmised. The core, where radioactive decay continues to provide energy, is still molten after billions of years. Driven by energy from below, molten rock even today wells up near the surface of both land and ocean areas. Volcanoes are only the most superficial signs of this upwelling, which is slowly but drastically changing the topology and making heavy elements available to us. Upwelling causes mountains to rise, though this doesn't happen overnight: figure on at least a few million years. The products of erosion from mountain heights may pile up to form the basis of a new mountain near the old one, or may be carried to considerable distances by some combination of wind, water, and gravity. So the surface at any point is moving up and down, constantly but slowly. Earth doesn't have life in the sense of being able to reproduce itself but it has its own slow way of being lively.

The upward movement of hot material is complemented by lateral movement of material that has cooled and solidified. Schoolchildren forced to study geography usually notice that they could cut out continents from a map – such abuse of a textbook may not be encouraged but it's easy to see what the result would be – and put them together like the pieces of a jigsaw puzzle. The west coast of Africa and Eurasia fits accurately onto the east coast of North, Central, and South America with a little hole that can be filled by Greenland. Greenland is actually a piece of North America, though it has moved so that it sits next to Europe.

Teachers in my schooldays made little of this match because it was hard to imagine something as big as a continent moving thousands of miles, but in this case what was obvious also turned out to be true. The term "continental drift," sometimes applied to this phenomenon, is a little misleading. The continents don't move as continents. Instead, fragments of the earth's broken crust called tectonic plates move at less than a snail's pace – typically an inch or two per year – across deeper supporting layers of the planet, carrying pieces of continent. Picture a ferryboat coming in to dock, moving at perhaps two miles per hour. Its collision with the dock occurs in slow motion, but the whole dock is moved and anything caught in between would be crushed. Tectonic plates move a billion times more slowly, but they have well over a billion times more mass than a ferryboat so nothing can stop them except collision with another plate.

This collision would take place over millions of years. Tectonic plate motion is the slowest motion I can think of. (Hair and fingernails also exhibit slow motion but they grow faster than tectonic plate movement, on average. Grass grows much faster.) Plates are driven by energy from the depths: the hot material coming up pushes them around. The plates and the pieces of continent they carry form and break up, to form again in different configurations hundreds of millions of years later. The continents we see today come from the disassembly of the giant supercontinent Pangaea two hundred million years ago in the Jurassic period. That's why Jurassic fossils discovered in Europe and North America are similar: two hundred million years ago these continents existed as adjacent parts of one large land mass with shared animal life. And there had been other supercontinents even earlier. Earth as we know it is thus a transient phase, as the slow tectonic dance goes on.[46]

The Beginning of Biology

Perhaps as much as three billion years ago chemistry on Earth got much more interesting. Certain unique groupings of atoms formed in the oceans, based on the elements hydrogen, nitrogen, oxygen, and carbon. Some of these groupings, or molecules, have also been found on the planet Mars, suggesting that this peculiar chemistry may have occurred throughout the universe. It is also possible, according to some scientists, that the primitive carbon-containing molecules were

46 Sometimes the dance is not so slow: the earthquakes that produced the tragic tsunamis of December, 2004 in the Indian Ocean and March, 2011 in the North Pacific represented the sudden release of energy from interacting tectonic plates. In each case the energy had been accumulated over millions of years but was released in seconds, like the snapping of a slowly stretched rubber band or the *twang* of a bowstring. Tectonic motion is slow on the average but is made up of such sudden jumps.

formed elsewhere and arrived on Earth as passengers on comets or asteroids. In any case these groups combined into increasingly complex molecules and finally took the big step: formation of entities that could replicate themselves. This is chemistry begetting the beginning of biology. Biology is the study of life.

The simple self-replicating entities of primitive biology evolved into more complex forms over time. There was far more to the development of humanity than Darwinian evolution through chemistry, but we focus for the moment on physical development of our species. Later we'll discuss development of culture, humanity, religion, and philosophy. They all depend on life, but life existed long before any of them. The increasingly complex life forms continued to reproduce themselves, eventually giving rise to all of the flora and fauna, including humankind, that inhabit Earth. It's a jump of billions of years from primitive organic molecules to Mozart, and creationists are fond of pointing out that not every step can be described in detail today. There is a lot we don't know yet, but that doesn't mean it won't eventually be explained within the broad evolutionary picture. Spectacular, varied, and beautiful as these developments were, it is important to note that even the biological processes of life did not violate any of the regular laws of physics and chemistry.

At bottom, the laws of chemistry are extraordinarily simple. Chemistry is based on interactions among atoms and molecules. These interactions are mediated by electric charge, which comes in two varieties, positive and negative. A single positive charge and a single negative charge have between them a net charge of zero. An atom normally has equal amounts of positive and negative charge, so its net charge adds up to zero, but the positive and negative charges are not mixed together. The positive charge is concentrated, with almost all of the mass, in the central nucleus. The nucleus contains protons, which have mass and charge; it also contains neutrons, which have mass but no charge. The positive charge of the protons in the nucleus is neutralized by the negative charge of the electrons, which form a cloud surrounding the nucleus. Electrons have very little mass but each electron in an atom has a charge of -1 in certain units.

The charge on each electron is always the same and is equal, though opposite in sign, to the charge on each proton; that is, each proton has a charge of +1. The number of electrons in an atom is equal to the number of protons in the nucleus. The universal rule governing charge is that like charges – two positive charges or two negative charges – repel each other, while opposite charges – a positive and a negative – attract each other.

The electrons can be pictured as traveling in orbits around the nucleus like planets in their orbits around the sun. The negative electrons are bound to the atom by their electrical attraction to the positive nucleus. They would be pulled into the nucleus but centrifugal force keeps them in their orbits, like clothes pressed against the spinning wall of a drier. The centrifugal force just balances the attraction of the nucleus and the electrons stay in their orbits. Electrical forces would push the positive charges in the nucleus apart – positive charges repel each other – but they are held together by another kind of force. This is the strong nuclear force, which is very powerful at short range but disappears at slightly longer range. Even the distance of the electrons from the nucleus would be too long a range for the nuclear force to operate, and besides the strong force does not act on electrons.

The cloud of electrons is 100,000 times larger in diameter than the nucleus, which can be considered a single point for most chemical purposes. Chemistry treats the nucleus mainly as a structureless charged mass at the center of the atom, so nuclear forces have little presence in chemistry. It's physicists who spend much of their time contemplating the internal structure of the nucleus. Right now we're talking about chemistry, which concentrates on the atomic electrons.

If two atoms are in the same vicinity their negative electron clouds repel each other. When the nearest electrons of the two atoms approach each other the positive charges of the nucleus have a much smaller effect, because they are so much farther away. At ordinary energies, the mutual repulsion of the electron clouds makes billiard balls collide with each other just the way billiard balls are supposed to. Repulsive forces between electrons give rise to the familiar behavior of everyday objects, which bounce off each other rather than merging. That's why you stand on the floor rather than sinking through it, even though you are being pulled downward by the gravitational attraction of Earth. The repulsion between the electrons of your feet and the electrons of the floor is strong enough to counter the gravitational pull of an entire planet.

Molecules and Organic Chemistry

In real life we don't usually encounter individual atoms. More often two or more atoms combine into a molecule, with electrons being transferred or shared between the atoms. The molecule is a distinct entity, with properties very different from the individual atoms. For example, one atom of the element sodium, which bursts into flame when placed in water, combines with one atom of the poisonous gas chlorine to make a molecule of common table salt, which is neither poisonous nor easy to burn. The electrons assume a configuration that holds the entity together. A molecule can be as simple as a combination of two atoms or as complex as a precise structure containing billions of atoms. Like charges repel, opposite charges attract: the results of these simple rules are extraordinarily complex – they include the processes of life itself – but there is no magic about them. Chemistry is merely the detailed study of the results of the interactions among electrons surrounding atomic nuclei.[47] These charged particles have no intelligence but respond primitively to the forces acting upon them.

The processes of life are processes of organic chemistry, the most complex branch of chemistry, which studies carbon-containing molecules. Organic molecules exist outside living things – plastics are examples of non-living organic substances – but life processes

---

47   Ok, I admit that I am oversimplifying for clarity. There are subtle quantum mechanical effects that condition the interactions of atoms and molecules, but they are not important to the argument. My point, that chemistry is the mindless elaboration of simple interactions, fortunately does not require us to explore the details of these subtle effects.

are usually part of the history. Plastics are often derived from refinement of petroleum, which is the residue of plant life from hundreds of millions of years ago. Still, the first organic molecules must have been formed before life began. Life, with its defining capacity for self-replication, dramatically multiplies the quantity of organic molecular matter. This is a huge effect. A very few self-replicating molecules, or perhaps only one, can lead over time to a dominant mass of similar molecules.

But despite its suggestive name, organic chemistry is governed by the same electrical forces as inorganic chemistry. Since chemistry remains chemistry, it should be no surprise that the chemistry of early living things interacted with that of the non-living planet. The emergence of life was a revolutionary factor in the chemical development of Earth. Today complicated life forms like mammals, fish, and birds take in oxygen and excrete carbon dioxide as one of many waste products. But earlier life forms, like plants today, produced oxygen as a waste product. The abundance of oxygen in our atmosphere results from chemical action of life forms that give off oxygen. At a stage of prehistory called the Permian, about a quarter of a billion years ago, a massive extinction of such life forms occurred. These dying organisms released their oxygen into the atmosphere in huge amounts. Rock contains a lot of iron. The iron tended to turn red at that time because it reacted chemically with the abundant oxygen, essentially forming rust (iron oxide), which is red. And layers of rock that formed at that time – Permian rock – still exhibit this redness very strikingly. When you see masses of red rock, you're probably looking at formations dating from a period of abundant oxygen. The chemistry of life was an element in the overall scheme of things, affecting the color of rock we see today by affecting its chemistry.

There is nothing inherently mysterious in the chemistry of life, nothing that cannot *in principle* be duplicated in a test tube. I have to say "in principle" because the organic molecules in living organisms are incredibly complex. Molecular biochemists have succeeded in directing chemical reactions involving DNA, one of the largest organic molecules. They have created new strands with different genetic properties, based on DNA retrieved from living organisms. But no one has yet created a strand of DNA *ab initio* from atomic components. A single cell is a concentrated chemistry laboratory containing many strands of DNA. Through intermediaries, the DNA strands regulate organic chemical reactions that determine the cell's function.

The Signature of Life

The DNA can make copies of itself (the process is sketched in Appendix B) which in turn allows the entire cell to reproduce. That ability is the unique signature of life. As complex as is everything going on in the minimal living organism that is a cell,[48] it can be represented as an interacting series of chemical reactions. Many of these reactions have been fully duplicated in test tubes and some day they all will be. These processes add up to life. The processes of life are beautiful consequences of the primitive processes of chemistry. They are miraculous – life is a miracle – in the sense that we contemplate them with awe and wonder. But God has not been required to do daily magic. The point of this discussion is that even life is accomplished through the mindless reactions of electrons to electrical forces.

Living things including human beings are perishable arrangements of the chemical elements. Shortly after death our bodies decompose. Atoms of hydrogen, carbon, oxygen, and the rest derived from a decomposed body do not differ from atoms of these elements derived elsewhere. Many atoms are replaced repeatedly by others of the same sort during our lives, and life goes on without interruption. Our humanity does not reside in the atoms that compose our bodies. The total quantity of each element in a human body has been measured. It would be easy to assemble corresponding amounts of each element

---

48 Actually a virus, which is a collection of bare DNA, is even more minimal than a cell. But a virus must live within some other host organism. More precisely, we should say that a cell is the minimal organism capable of independent living.

and mix them in a pot, but this would not produce a human being or even a fruit fly. The elements – more than a trillion trillion atoms – would have to be precisely arranged into molecules, folded into defined shapes, and twisted into incredible combinations.

But while the job is long it is not infinite. After all, we know that it was accomplished within the four billion year history of Earth. It could and undoubtedly will be repeated in a much shorter time in human laboratories. Instructions for doing it could in principle be compiled into a manual which would be a representation of the pattern that turns a shelf full of elements into a living organism looking much like you or me. This manual, which would be very long, in some sense represents the difference between a few dollars' worth of chemicals and a living being. The key to human life is contained in the *arrangement* of a human's constituents, not in the constituents themselves. There is no unique constituent in a living body. There is only the same stuff that makes up everything else.

Humans have emerged in the latest few millionths of the time since t_0. We are made of garden-variety elements combined by processes that obey garden-variety physical and chemical laws. We are highly complex, but there is nothing special about us from a physical or chemical point of view. And yet, so far as we know we are the most completely fulfilled portion of God's creation. If even the chemistry of life is a matter of charges attracting and repelling each other, the nature of our uniqueness must reside in something other than the very ordinary clay of which we are formed. Life is more than chemistry. We saw that the meaning of being was not contained in the physics that caused the earth to form. We expressed a suspicion that the meaning of being might be related to the meaning of life, but now we find that the meaning of life is not contained in the chemistry of living organisms. We have discussed the chemistry of life, but life is more than chemistry. And the meaning of humanity is deeper still: there was life for billions of years before humans appeared on the scene. God has created us: given us being. We must be important to him. If our significance does not lie in our chemistry, where does it reside?

CHAPTER 6:
Living Software

I may have outraged some people when I suggested that from a limited perspective we can be viewed as sacks of chemicals undergoing very ordinary reactions. This doesn't seem to provide a basis for anything that could be described as a spiritual life. Can a sack of chemicals search for meaning or respond to love? There must be something more to us than chemicals. We must have a seat of meaning. Life is chemistry, but it can't *only* be chemistry.

It has not always been clear that even our chemistry falls within the bounds of natural law, that life can be created from non-living material. There is still controversy about this question. One of the most famous experiments on the subject was devoted to that despised creature, the maggot, which is the larva of an insect. A good reason you don't leave raw meat or fish lying around without refrigeration is that if you do, maggots will soon make themselves apparent. The long-held hypothesis had been that rotten meat formed maggots by "spontaneous generation." This notion was refuted by the experiment of the Italian physician Francesco Redi (1626-1697). In his experiment Redi placed samples of meat or fish in jars. Some of the jars were open while others were covered by fine gauze that prevented insects or their eggs from entering. Soon plenty of maggots were observed in the uncovered jars but none in the jars with gauze covering. Conclusion: the maggots in the uncovered jars were the result of eggs laid by flies, not of spontaneous generation. This conclusion was generalized to the principle, *omne vivum ex ovo*: all life from the egg, the refutation of spontaneous generation.

Creationists love this generalized principle because they claim it proves their point. If you talk about organic molecules evolving into living organisms they will tell you Redi proved that spontaneous generation is impossible. Since life cannot arise spontaneously, God must have performed a specific miracle to get the process started. This is a classic example of wishful overinterpretation. In fact Redi's experiment showed only that raw meat does not spontaneously produce maggots. It was a brilliantly simple demonstration and is still used to teach school children the principles of the scientific method, but it did not prove that the most primitive life forms could not evolve from non-living material.

The creationists are wrong. Life is not a miracle in the sense of a suspension of ordinary natural law. The chemistry of life arises continuously from ordinary chemistry, whose laws are particular cases of the laws of physics. We can aspire to grasp these laws. Though complex and beautiful, they are by no means beyond our eventual comprehension. We know a great deal about the chemistry of life, and though we do not fully understand life's chemical processes today the time is quickly approaching when we will be able to take control of them. There is nothing about life's chemical processes that violates the laws governing all chemical processes. There is no magic in our chemistry, nothing that cannot in principle be duplicated in a test tube.

Life and Humanity

In saying this, I am not being reductive. I am speaking of life in the most basic terms, of life that is a combination of molecules showing the ability to replicate itself. Life that behaves in a spiritual manner, life that stands in awe before a sunset, or a waterfall, or a painting, or a symphony, life that gropes toward God, is a far deeper mystery. This is the point I am working toward. Life as a chemical phenomenon is already amazing, already something to celebrate. But in the end the chemistry is ordinary, finite, comprehensible. That can't be where meaning resides; chemistry is not what responds to God's love.

As more and more of the processes of life are understood in detail, the moment approaches when living organisms will be created in the laboratory. Creation of life will not be limited to the likes of cloning, in which the starting material is derived from living organisms. Before too much longer – surely within the present millennium and perhaps the present decade – the processes that produced us will be repeated in the laboratory. Living organisms will be created from simple reagents, as happened when life originally developed. The profound mystery of life does not reside in its chemical processes. The connection between the miracle of humanity and the mundane chemical nature of life lies elsewhere.

That the chemistry of life is mundane is an insight of the twentieth century. In 1818, when Mary Wollstonecraft Shelley's Dr. Frankenstein wanted to create life, his starting material comprised salvaged cadaveric parts. Motion picture adaptations show him channeling an uncontrollable bolt of lightning into a dead body to animate his monster. The monster in turn was wild, terrifying, nightmarish. The story warns us not to trifle with forbidden mysteries.

We now understand that life is an elaboration of describable, repeatable organic chemistry. God did not need anything magical to create life; he did it in warm seas with a natural broth of simple carbon-containing molecules. (See: we were in hot water right from the start.) He may or may not have used a bolt of lightning – this is one form of catalyst that has been postulated – but lightning is an electrical phenomenon that has been duplicated in laboratories. You can experience it by flying a kite in a thunderstorm, but I don't recommend it: Ben Franklin was lucky. We can't quite reproduce the first steps in biological chemistry today, but we're a lot closer than Frankenstein was. Our understanding is growing exponentially, and test tube generation of life will soon be possible. It is quite another question whether it is desirable for us to have such an ability. Many would argue that our civilization is not ready for it, even though we might use this power to accomplish great things. But ready or not, we *will* have the power and we will create living creatures. No divine spark, nothing mysterious, is required. The chemistry of life is mundane even though its results are not.

We spoke in Chapter 5 of unique groupings of atoms that formed in the oceans and combined into molecules that could replicate themselves: the first living things. The simplest organisms evolved into others trillions of times more complex, still based on the same chemistry, and these organisms eventually became the progenitors of mammals like us. As mammals we are the product of primordial broth and a few billion years' evolution. Our life processes are not fundamentally different from chemical processes that are carried out in a test tube; if we have a form of divinity it does not lie in special chemistry. Even the chemistry of human life is mundane, though in non-chemical ways the transition to humanity is a heroic leap.

The often-heard statement that life begins at conception is misleading in two different ways. Life begins long before conception. A skin cell, a sperm cell, an egg cell, a tumor cell: all have life. The chemistry of life is continuous from the earliest times on a solid Earth billions of years ago. But the same cannot be said of humanity: that's a much more recent development. When a human egg and a sperm cell meet and combine, the resulting entity is called a zygote. As a blood cell or a hair follicle is not a person, neither the egg nor the sperm cell is in any sense a person. And a zygote is not a person. This is the second sense in which it is misleading to state that life begins at conception: the zygote, like the egg cell and the sperm cell, is alive but is not a person.

The combination of egg and sperm results in catalysis of a series of ordinary chemical reactions, the product of which is a cluster of two, then four, and eventually many cells. A cluster smaller than the period at the end of this sentence is called a blastocyst. It consists of perhaps a hundred undifferentiated cells. In contrast, a baby has trillions of cells of many differently specialized types. The blastocyst is a purely chemical entity: it has no organs, no memories, no aspirations. It experiences neither joy nor suffering: it has no consciousness. It has no way of knowing or caring what happens to it and no way to remember anything: it knows nothing. It cannot seek God. Though it is a chemical marvel, to speak of this cluster of cells as an embryo may mislead by conjuring the picture of a very small baby. The blastocyst is not any kind of baby; it is a formless globe, without humanity. Despite its potential, the suggestion that the blastocyst is a person with a human soul is absurd and deceptive. The blastocyst is a mundane consequence of the laws of chemistry. The soul, the personal life, the humanity – the appearance, for the first time, of a unique individual – they come later.

What eventually gives meaning to higher life forms like human beings is something other than chemistry. To understand it, we need to engage in a digression. We start simply, with the definition of a circle.

Eternal Pi

A circle includes all the points in a plane – a flat surface – that lie at a given distance, called the radius, from a reference point, the center. Since by definition all points on the circle are the same distance from the center, all radii are exactly equal. The length of a line drawn from a point on the circle, through the center, and to the opposite point on the circle is the diameter. A diameter includes two radii, so the diameter is twice the radius and all diameters are also exactly equal. The distance around the circle, starting at any point and returning to that same point, is the circumference.

If you lay out a piece of string along the circle, cut it to length, and then straighten it out along a ruler, you can measure the circumference. You can cut another piece of string to the length of the diameter. Comparing the two, you would find that the circumference string was somewhat more than three times the length of the diameter string: in fact, a bit more than 3.1 times longer but less than 3.2 times. Successively more accurate measurements would show that this ratio is more than 3.14 but less than 3.15; more than 3.141 but less than 3.142; more than 3.1415 but less than 3.1416. You quickly get beyond the point where you can make the measurements accurately enough to keep filling in decimal places, but mathematicians have ways to continue the calculation without measurements. This ratio of the circumference to the diameter is called "pi," represented by the Greek letter π, and is equal to 3.14159… and so forth.

Mathematicians find that two remarkable statements can be made about this ratio:

First: no matter how many decimal places you go to you never reach the exact value of π. There are an infinite number of decimal places, approximating π more and more closely but never quite exactly, no matter how many places are filled in.

Second: π, the ratio of the circumference to the diameter, is always exactly the same, no matter how big or small the circle.

Always the same, never expressible as a normal number. It's quite mysterious, and it's a constant inconvenience, but it's a fact of life that the ratio π is what it is. Nothing can be done to change it.

At least you might think so. Actually, I heard somewhere that a certain state legislature decided, many years ago, that this value was unwieldy and too difficult for the children in its schools. Like King Canute, the legislature decided to change natural law by fiat.[49] Thenceforth, π in that state was to equal exactly three. Never mind that if you laid out a circle with string, the length of string used in going around the outside of the circle was more than three times the length in going across the center of the circle. And never mind that engineering calculations, for example, would all be wrong: bridges would collapse, roads would not meet. The standard value was too awkward to be tolerated. So the legislature did what God could not. They changed the value of π.

For the rest of us π remains what is called an irrational number, which means it cannot be expressed as the quotient of two integers.[50] It is possible to fill in a great many of its decimal places; the last I heard computers had been used to calculate the first five trillion of them. (Don't ask me why.) But there will always be more places than have been calculated. The integers in successive decimal places go on forever and their values are fixed: calculable though not yet calculated. It is impossible to draw a circle for which π will be different in any decimal place.

---

49 Actually, the story is that Canute ordered the tide to recede in order to show his sycophantic courtiers that he did *not* have this power. He was apparently brighter than his state legislature.

50 For many practical purposes a simple approximation as 22/7 is accurate enough; it's too large only by about 0.04%. But no quotient of two integers can ever express π exactly.

The quantity π existed from the beginning of time and had its present value – *all* decimal places, out to infinity – before anyone ever drew a circle. It is an inherent property of circles: God himself could not have made circles in this universe with a different value of π. The infinite sequence of numbers that make up π is ancient and immutable. It never has been and never will be represented in its entirety on paper or computer storage, so it cannot be said to be stored anywhere, though it can be deduced from the known properties of a circle. Thus while π is nowhere in space, is unaffected by time, and has nothing to do with chemistry, it has its own stable existence. You can't touch it, but it's real.

Software and Sweaters

Now let us consider another example of something with these properties. The world of computers is populated by two types of entity: hardware and software. Roughly speaking, hardware includes everything chemical, everything you could hold in your hand: computers, cables, modems, even storage media like disks and tapes and flash memories. Software is the information that animates the system: the set of operations it is instructed to perform. I will use the word "software" to mean the program – the information – itself, rather than its representation on a storage medium. Despite its gentle name, software is more durable than hardware. Hardware can be damaged easily, by a blow, or immersion, or heat, for example. You'd better not drop your computer; you might have to spend a thousand dollars for a new one. Hardware is usually delivered with a specified operating temperature range and is not guaranteed to work outside that range.

Software, on the other hand, is immune to damage. When a program is said to have been corrupted, what is meant is that the *representation* has been changed. A copy of the program might have been stored in a computer, where unauthorized changes to the copy could occur. Or it could have been stored on a disk that was subsequently melted in a fire. Melting the disk does not harm the software as long as there are other disks containing the program: the original program would still exist, though it could no longer be read from the melted disk. There is no operating temperature range for software. If you have hardware that will operate in the frosts of Antarctica or the heat of the interior of the sun, your software will work fine. You can keep as many backup copies of your software disk as you like, in case some of them become damaged. As I'm using the term, software, like the ratio π, is nowhere in space, is unaffected by time, and has nothing to do with chemistry, but has real and stable existence.

A software program is a pattern, like the pattern for knitting a sweater. In its most basic form it is an arrangement of 0's and 1's; each 0 or 1 is called a "bit." If a simple program, to make up a random example, is 01001101, the pattern can be stated in words: "The first element (i.e. 0), then the second (i.e. 1), then the first twice, then the second twice, then the first, then the second." If 0 stands for "knit" and 1 stands for "purl", this program could actually be used as a knitting pattern. The first 0 and 1 would be read "knit, purl." The entire program would be, "knit, purl, knit, knit, purl, purl, knit, purl", or "knit one, purl one, knit two, purl two, knit one, purl one." The program is not the sweater, but specifies how to make the sweater. Anyone who knows how can knit the sweater from this pattern, and the sweaters will all come out the same. You can knit a program into a sweater like Madame Defarge.

A real program looks just like our example,[51] though it's generally longer. I've written useful programs as short as five thousand bits; some programs are shorter while others can exceed a billion bits. Regardless of the length it is the pattern that supplies the meaning, just as it's the arrangement of letters that distinguishes Shakespeare's *Hamlet* from a collection of random strokes on a typewriter, though the same alphabet is used in each case. It doesn't matter at all that

---

51 Computer programs as humans create and manipulate them use "languages" that combine many bits into instructions we can understand, to make programming easier. But the fundamental program as the computer processes it is a string of 0's and 1's.

the elements we worked with were 0 and 1; the 0 and 1 are just the alphabet. It's the arrangement that counts. The same arrangement with a different alphabet – say, ABAABBAB – is *exactly* the same program: a sweater knitted from it, with A and B standing for "knit" and "purl", will be identical to one knitted from the program with 0's and 1's. A representation of a program stored on paper (this page, for example) or some other storage medium can be destroyed or changed, but the program has an independent existence in the same way that the equation $2 + 2 = 4$ exists independent of the fact that I just wrote it down.[52] It was true that two plus two equals four before there were humans to note this fact. The different representations of the pattern above illustrate the crucial point: patterns are independent of the objects they arrange. The pattern is not the bits. The alphabet must have at least two elements, and two elements is the common approach in computer work, but it could have more. The software of cells, sketched in Appendix B, uses an alphabet with four elements.

A software program is a pattern. But while the digits of π, or the sum of two and two, are fixed beyond our control, a software program represents a pattern that someone has created. Unlike π it is not eternal: it exists only from the time of its creation. It can be modified: it can grow and it usually does. Most programs are developed in phases, a little at a time, and each phase can operate as if it were the finished program. In fact it's often hard to say when a program is finished; what usually happens is that someone thinks of additional useful features to be added. So the program grows some more. A program can be represented on computer disks but it is not destroyed if disks are thrown into a furnace. The simple pattern 01001101 set out above could be copied a million times, transmitted

---

52 It's hard to argue that the program would exist if *all* representations – all storage disks containing the program, for example – were destroyed. But if there was just one representation, its utility would not be compromised by the fact that any number of other storage disks had been destroyed. Even if all the disks were destroyed but someone remembered the details of the program, it could still be made available.

all over the globe, and broadcast into outer space. The pattern that is the software, once it has been created, exists on its own.

Meaning in Molecules

We engaged in this digression to make an important point. A computer would be little more than a useless collection of silicon chips without software, which is the basis of meaning in a computer. In the same way, living organisms, including mammals like us, would not exist as organisms without our own software. Our software is not stored in a single place like a computer disk or memory. Instead, it manifests itself throughout our bodies in the pattern of arrangement of our molecules. The molecules themselves, as we saw above, are no more than chemical phenomena. A random collection of molecules will not function as an organism. The molecules are interesting but not in themselves significant. The organization, the pattern of their arrangement, is another matter. The alphabet we all write with was a remarkable but limited achievement. A randy fraternity member might arrange the letters of that alphabet to compose a bawdy limerick. Shakespeare could arrange them to create *Hamlet*. In the same way, our molecular *patterns* lead to something of a very different order from the sum of our *molecules*.

The software of life begins with the genes we inherit from our parents, but it is expanded by every experience of our lives. The genetic inheritance resides in the chromosomes, a collection of very complex single molecules. Each chromosome contains within itself a pattern of great meaning. The pattern is not the chromosomes, but it specifies how to make them. The chromosomes in turn define how to make the organism. The chromosomes tell the blastocyst how to develop into a more complex organism. The presence of a pattern is the most obvious thing about the chromosomes, which contain the program for making a living organism and define the organism's starting point. The starting point sets some limits. Though life's experiences create vast changes in the organism, no baby born to human parents will develop ears like a donkey or a tail like a horse, and no colt born to horses will learn to read.

But the organism defined by DNA from human parents starts as a blank slate. Many identical organisms can be started from duplicated DNA, but at this point they are certainly not persons, not individuals, not unique. The organism is an arrangement of chemicals, as *Hamlet* is an arrangement of letters. When the pattern is applied to the chemicals, they begin to act together as a living organism. Then life expands the pattern. An organism can not only reproduce; it can learn. As its various experiences produce a true individual, the organism becomes a human being.

It may be useful to review the software-driven chemistry. A chromosome is a molecule of deoxyribonucleic acid (DNA). The program is encoded directly onto the molecule. The order in which certain chemical entities are placed on the long strands of the chromosome represents the pattern: the program for assembling the organism. The characteristics called for by the program are built into the embryo. It is very important that the DNA containing the molecular program itself is also built into the organism. The DNA molecule is so arranged that a copy can be made, eventually allowing the organism to make others like itself as the molecule with its program is reproduced.

The ability of the DNA molecule to form identical copies of itself is the basis for the reproduction of living organisms. It is the pattern – the software – that is reproduced, not the individual atoms or the individual strands of DNA. Each sperm cell contains the father's DNA pattern, while each egg contains the mother's. When a sperm cell fertilizes an egg, the DNA patterns from the two parents are combined. The DNA, which transmits the pattern from the two parents, produces mixed inheritance encoded into the DNA of the resulting zygote. The DNA molecule is a chemical entity, but it can be understood to be simply a medium for storing a long[53] program. The software is dominant.

---

53 The program on one chromosome is tens of millions of units long: longer than *Hamlet* and all the other plays of Shakespeare combined. It takes a massive pattern to define the starting point of an organism.

Beyond DNA

The DNA contains the software describing the organism's genetic inheritance: a sort of t_0 condition for this organism. As the organism develops the total pattern goes far beyond the t_0 pattern expressed by the chromosomes. Sometimes two or more identical blastocysts are produced. Each, if it survives, will become a distinct individual. Even identical twins, with the same DNA, are distinct individuals because their life experiences, beginning in the womb, are never identical. From conception, even during the prenatal period, things happen to the organism. Every experience of life produces changes, not in the DNA but in the overall software. Just as a computer program can grow by having additional features added to it, the software of an organism grows.

Because of its genetic heritage the organism has the capacity to learn, to change. Experiments have shown that when a newborn kitten opens its eyes the arrangement of neurons – the pattern of molecules – in its brain is physically changed by the visual stimuli presented. If you show the kitten horizontal lines, its brain will always thereafter respond in a special way to seeing horizontal lines. Similarly, when a child learns that C follows B that fact is somehow encoded in the molecules of his brain, becoming a part of his chemical makeup via a change in the molecular pattern. Although children are the most pliable – the best learners – the process is not limited to children. It never ends during our sentient lives. A physical change in the pattern of molecules in your brain has resulted from reading the preceding sentences, regardless of whether you agree, disagree, don't understand, or don't care.

Even when the molecules themselves are physically replaced by new ones, the knowledge is preserved because something in the *pattern* retains it: the new molecules retain the pattern. For a human organism, the experiences of life range from earliest bonding with a parent to fading in old age, and everything that is encountered in between. Schooling, nutrition, trauma, joy, sights, sounds, smells: all contribute to the formation of the individual by changing the overall pattern of the organism. Every experience becomes an element in the individual's humanity. This effect is seen most notably in the brain but every portion of the body's pattern is significant.

These experiences, important as they are to the organism's humanity, usually do not affect the DNA. The DNA does not define a human being; it merely defines the substrate organism that may *become* a human being. When the DNA replicates itself and an offspring organism is produced, initially that organism has yet to become human. The changes resulting from experiences are not passed on genetically to succeeding generations, though of course succeeding generations learn from their predecessors. Even though you have learned to read, your children are not born with this ability; they'll have to learn reading for themselves. So each individual is unique, though the genetic basis provides a starting point that is set entirely by the code contained within the DNA.

For the most part the DNA coding is unchanged for life, but there are things that can produce alterations called mutations. For example, radiation can break a molecule of DNA which may then repair itself incorrectly. When that molecule replicates itself the new molecules will propagate this error. Some kinds of toxic material have a similar effect. Accidents like these can result in faulty DNA, with two possible serious results. One is that the faulty DNA may cause the cells containing it to undergo uncontrolled growth: cancer, which may kill the organism. Alternatively, if the mutation occurs in cells involved in reproduction the changed DNA can be incorporated into an offspring organism, which may be nonviable or may be born with a genetic disease.

It is also possible, though *much* less common, that the mutation is favorable. Classic examples include mutations presumably leading to a longer neck for a giraffe that succeeds by eating leaves high on a tree – imagine the advantage of being able to eat leaves your competitors can't reach – or, for Darwin's finches, a strong beak to help an organism that lives by cracking seeds. Mutation in the DNA is the basis for evolutionary development of species, in an extension of Darwin's theory beyond what he could have known. It is the DNA program that evolves. Darwin's finches developed beaks adapted to their food supply as numerous small mutations were reinforced. The mutations were passed on only if they helped make the organisms fit for survival in the conditions they encountered; the vast majority of mutations are insignificant or deadly and these mutations are not reinforced. Mutation can be good for the species in the very long run – we consider ourselves an improvement over the long-extinct creatures from which we evolved – but it is most often tragic for the individual. Generally speaking, mutations are passed on to subsequent generations in the rare cases where they improve the ability to survive. The majority of mutations hinder survival, and offspring inheriting them lose out in the competition, often dying before birth.

Body and Soul

I recently heard an evangelical anti-abortion speaker argue that the fetus, from the instant of conception, is "biologically human." I think he's on the wrong track. Humanity as we have been discussing it is not just a question of biology. From the instant of conception the fetus is biologically *homo sapiens*, our species. But at conception it is incapable of characteristic human activities. Early *homo sapiens* is dramatically labeled among other things by symbolic thinking demonstrated in cave art, statues, shell beads, incised ochre, pendants, and figurines. *Homo sapiens* was probably the first species to develop spoken language. The fetus initially has no behavior at all, and certainly no symbolic activity.

We have seen that the beginning of the pattern of a living organism is based on its genetic inheritance through the coding of its DNA. Whether it's descended from a fruit fly or a human being, the organism develops in response to every experience. A blastocyst resulting from two human parents can develop into a human being, but the blastocyst is not itself a human being. A description of discarding a blastocyst as tantamount to killing a baby is outrageous. Humanity develops through experiences. A blastocyst has experienced nothing and remembers nothing. It is not a human being. A newborn baby must be considered a human being. The transition from blastocyst to baby is gradual; it doesn't seem possible to assign a first instant when the organism is human. This may be an important question for lawyers or legislators to answer, but I can't do more than state that a blastocyst falls short of the line, and a baby at birth has crossed it. The total pattern never stops developing, growing, as long as the individual remains alive and conscious.

Our understanding of the kind of cellular programming seen in DNA and other molecules is expanding very rapidly. Sooner than we might think, we will be able to make a living organism, starting from jars of inorganic reagents. All that distinguishes jars of reagents from living organisms is the pattern of arrangement of the constituent atoms. The pattern itself has no chemistry, but it arranges the chemical elements that make up the organism. A hundred jars of reagents – there are only about that many natural elements – provide everything needed to make Shakespeare, Hitler, or Mother Theresa. The same elements in each case! Every play and sonnet embedded in Shakespeare's mind, every obscene notion Hitler was infected with, every impulse of humanity Mother Theresa felt, was encoded in molecular patterns: software. It is the pattern, not the molecules, that makes the difference; they all had similar molecules. The pattern started with a genetic inheritance and developed throughout the lives of these dramatically different individuals. Just as π existed and had its present value before anyone ever drew a circle, so the software that defines Mother Theresa can exist independent of the molecules of her decomposing clay. As a program transcends the chemistry of the medium that stores it, Mother Theresa transcends the chemistry of the body she inhabited.

Humans are made of identically the same elements that form all normal matter. Biology, the study of the combination of molecules into life forms, can be seen as a branch of chemistry, the study of how atoms and molecules interact. Life processes do not require any rewriting of the laws of physics. The chemistry of life is not yet fully understood, but no chemical reaction occurs in life that cannot take place in a test tube under the right conditions. It is our software that defines our humanity. We have at last reached something that is not mundane: the software.

This software, this pattern, this arrangement begins with our genetic inheritance and grows each instant with our experiences of life. So far as we know it is the culmination and purpose of God's creation. The software is not the organism. The software exists independent of the elements it arranges. It has no location in space and time, though its embodiment is localized. It is indestructible, weightless, undetectable by any chemical test or by dissection of the body. When the body dies the software cannot be seen leaving the body. Yet the software animates the body. The word animate comes from the Latin *anima*, soul.

The software is the soul.

By itself the soul can do nothing. It animates the body; it must be associated with some sort of body. There are kinds of computer program that are written to be portable. That means that the program can be used on different kinds of computers. But there is no program that can be used by itself without something to animate. Similarly, the soul is not free-floating. But it may well be portable: there is no reason the soul cannot transcend the dissolution of the body, providing that there is another, not necessarily identical, body for it to animate. The third part of the Nicene Creed speaks of the resurrection of the dead. Alternative translations speak of the resurrection of the *body*. This does not have to mean that the dead person's body rises up; we know that the body remains in this world at death and that, over the years, its molecules are scattered. But if the soul of John Jones from Akron is translated to a new body, it need not become some sort of amorphous contribution to the allness of the universe. The individual is recognizable, even in the new body. It knows itself to be John Jones, formerly of Akron, now existing in a different plane of being.

The software is the soul of the individual, the part that can respond to God's message. Our humanity, our meaning, lies in our software. Software equals soul.

CHAPTER 7:
The Word

After some point in the second decade of our life, most of us stop growing taller. (It takes an effort of will for some of us to stop growing wider, but that's another story.) Yet the soul is still able to grow. We have seen that the soul is the part of us that can respond to God. And what is his message; what is the meaning we are trying to receive?

To get closer to the question of meaning, we're going to think a bit about time. Our word "time" has at least two counterparts in Greek. *Chronos* means time as measured by a clock. *Kairos* is a more subtle concept, something like "the fullness of time" or "time pregnant with meaning" or "the time of opportunity." Luke says "The time came for her (Mary) to deliver her child."[54] We understand *chronos*, but perhaps *kairos* points toward something less rigid, closer to the eternal.

Although there has always been being there has not always been time, at least in the sense of *chronos*. Being is not limited by time: it is eternal, since God, the ground of being, is eternal. I am going to cite authority stating that meaning is also eternal. But our universe is not eternal: it's about fourteen billion years old. This raises the question of how eternal being and eternal meaning can relate to our temporal universe: what does eternity have to do with time?

God created time when he created the universe. Genesis speaks of the beginning of time: "*In the beginning* when God created the heavens and the earth..." While we can say that God always exists, we cannot say that he existed for an infinite time before creating the universe. Before the creation of the universe there was no time. We

---

54 Luke 2:6

mentioned in Chapter 3 that time, like space, is a property of this universe. No universe, no time: this is a new insight, first proposed by Albert Einstein a little over a century ago.

Mutable Time

Before Einstein time was pretty much taken for granted and was assumed to be something inert, something inherent in being. But Einstein deduced that time, like space, is mutable. If you are traveling very much faster than I, your measurements of time will not be the same as mine. The difference does not result from any effect of speed on the mechanism of your watch. If you slow down, our watches will run at the same speed once again; your watch will still work as well as it ever did. It is not your watch, but *time itself*, that is affected by speed. The slowing of time at high speeds is called time dilation. It sounds hopelessly theoretical and it is – for ordinary speeds. Even for the motion of a rifle bullet, one of the fastest speeds we normally encounter, time is changed only by around two parts in a trillion. Earth's orbital motion around the sun changes time by less than five parts in a billion. Unless you approach the speed of light, which is about a million times faster than a rifle bullet, time dilation is present but is too small to measure.

An example of what time dilation means is the famous twin paradox. Suppose Jeff and Jim are identical twins aged twenty years. Jeff goes off for a long ride on a very fast space ship, traveling at nearly the speed of light. His objective is a star known to be twenty-five light years away. Remember that a light year is a measure of distance, equal to a little under six trillion miles. Jeff reaches the star, turns around, and returns to Earth. A little over fifty years after Jeff set out, Jim leads a big crowd to greet him. When Jeff steps out of his ship the onlookers are amazed. Jim is marked by his seventy years while his identical twin is still a young man in his twenties! Time dilation, the slowing of time, has caused Jeff to age much less than Jim. From Jeff's point of view the trip has taken only a few years, though it covered a round-trip distance of fifty light years. In fact Jeff feels that he has time traveled: moved fifty years into a future where his brother is now an old man.

It still sounds theoretical, but this is not a fable. It is what would actually happen if we had a space ship that could travel that fast for that long. We don't, of course, and I doubt that we ever will. But don't conclude that what I have described can never be observed. It's possible to demonstrate time dilation experimentally, though since we cannot travel at anything approaching the speed of light we can't do the experiment with wrist watches, or twins. Subtler techniques are needed. One that is quite simple to explain[55] concerns certain elementary particles that, once created, exist for only a very short time: typically less than a billionth of a second.

Each of these particles ends its life by spontaneously disintegrating. But it can't *just* disappear because it has mass. We saw in Chapter 5 that the total of mass and energy combined never changes, so the particle that disintegrated has to be replaced by other particles, or by energy in the form of radiation, or by both. These replacements can be detected in the lab, providing a signal that the original particle has disintegrated at a certain point and a certain time.

The time before a specific particle disintegrates cannot be predicted, but in a sample of two thousand particles one can say on the basis of measurements that one thousand will disintegrate before a given time. Insurance companies make this kind of calculation all the time. Though they have no idea when a given individual will die, actuaries will confidently calculate that in a cohort of forty-year-old men a predictable number will live at least thirty more years and will therefore not collect on their thirty-year term policies. Insurance rates are set on the basis of these calculations. Similarly, in a statistical sense the particle has a measureable lifetime.

Suppose we use a particle accelerator – many such devices exist and are in daily use – to accelerate particles to the speeds we desire. First we produce a group of particles at a comparatively low speed where time dilation has little effect. We measure how long they take to disintegrate, giving us the lifetime of that particle. Now we repeat

55 The experiment is simple only in principle. The details are fairly complex but we don't need to worry about them. The experiment has been performed in many laboratories. The result is as described.

these measurements with another group of particles, but this time we accelerate them to nearly the speed of light. We measure the lifetime of these fast particles, expecting it to be the same as the lifetime of the slow particles of the first group. Since all the particles are identical we expect the two groups to have identical lifetimes, but we're in for a surprise. The lifetime for the fast particles is longer than for the slow particles. Going at nearly the speed of light, they experience time dilation and their lifetimes are increased, just like Jeff the traveling twin. It's true: when a particle is going at nearly the speed of light it actually lives longer than it would at a slower speed. The particle is still the same; it is *time itself* that has been changed. This is a real experiment and has been performed in real laboratories.

Experiments like this show directly that time, as experienced by the particle, has slowed down. Time dilation causes a change in the particle's lifetime, and the change is exactly equal to that predicted by Einstein. By the way, it need not be a small effect: at energies achievable in large accelerators, a particle's lifetime could be extended substantially. Take as an example a particle with a lifetime of one billionth of a second. If we accelerate it to ninety-nine percent of the speed of light, it would have a lifetime of fourteen billionths of a second.

We see that time, like space, is a real, changeable thing, a property unique to our universe, not an inherent part of being. Our universe is immersed in time and bound by it, but outside our universe time has no meaning.

Manifest Meaning in the Time-Bound Universe

We were talking about time and eternity. While "before the creation of the universe" doesn't have a well-defined meaning, we can speak of a state with no universe and no time. This state also has no space: space, like time, is special to our universe. But the ground of being exists eternally, whether the universe exists or not. As its first order of business, the Gospel of John speaks of meaning and makes it clear that meaning is also eternal:

In the beginning was the Word, and the Word was with God, and the Word was God. He was in the beginning with God. All things came into being through him, and without him not one thing came into being. What has come into being through him was life, and the life was the light of all people. The light shines in the darkness, and the darkness did not overcome it.[56]

Like all the scriptural quotations used here, the passage is given as translated into English. John's Gospel was written in Greek so its author uses the Greek word *logos*, which the English version translates as *word. Logos* means

the divine wisdom manifest in the creation, government, and redemption of the world and often identified with the second person of the Trinity[57]

In other words, as God is the ground of being, the Word is the meaning of being. Here at last we approach an explicit answer to the question of meaning. The opening words of the Gospel of John emphasize that the Word was not created when the universe was created. He[58] was already there at the beginning of time. John tells us that the Word – the meaning – is eternal, as the ground of being is eternal. Through him has come "the light of all people." He was with God and he was God. God and his Word: eternal being and its eternal meaning.

So meaning was already present when the universe was created. We saw in Chapter 4 that from the theist's perspective the universe was created to be a home for humankind. (I don't mean to restrict "humankind" to Earth's furless mammalian bipeds; the term encompasses all sentient, autonomous, self-aware creatures that may inhabit the universe.) Early humans searched for meaning and the tentative answers they found gradually evolved into religion. Then, very recently everything changed. The meaning, already present at the creation of the universe fourteen billion years ago, manifested himself

---

56 John 1:1-5

57 Merriam-Webster's Collegiate Dictionary,

© 1994 Merriam-Webster, Inc.

58 As the Word, equivalent to the Son of God, is a person of the Trinity, we follow scripture in using the pronoun "he" rather than "it." Again we use this male form without suggesting that the Word has a gender.

in our time-bound universe. Christians believe that the central event of history occurred when the Word was made flesh. It happened an instant ago compared to geologic times. Somehow, meaning became incarnate – clothed in human flesh – in the man Jesus of Nazareth. Jesus as the Christ is the incarnation of the meaning of being. The incarnation is a distinct historic occurrence with a date. We don't know the date exactly – it wasn't December 25, 0001 – but it was about two thousand years ago. By comparison with the fourteen billion year-old universe the incarnation is a current event. It is the unique intersection of the eternal with the temporal.

The Parting of the Veil

Luke paints a picture of celestial wonders at the time of the birth of Jesus:

And suddenly there was with the angel a multitude of the heavenly host, praising God and saying, "Glory to God in the highest heaven, and on earth peace among those whom he favors!" [59]

We see that, this one time, the veil is parted and a direct connection is established between temporal Earth and eternal Heaven.[60] That is the core of the Christmas narrative. In Paul's words,

So if anyone is in Christ, there is a new creation; everything old has passed away; see, everything has become new! [61]

We are privileged to live in the very time of that miraculous happening, the New Being ushered in by Jesus, our contemporary.

The miracles described in Chapter 3, like the emergence of grain from the ground or the emergence of life from chemicals in the sea, are wonders of a nature that we can appreciate and begin to understand. We are now in the presence of a different meaning of the word "miracle." In this case the miracle is more than a mere wonder. It is not a divine magic act, nor is it technology that we can aspire to comprehend, much less duplicate. The incarnation of meaning – not

---

59 Luke 2:13-14

60 This insight is from a Christmas sermon by
Mother Madelyn K. Johnston

61 2 Corinthians 5:17

just the meaning of life but the meaning of being itself – in a human is unique. The uniqueness is not a mere matter of scale, like the difference between, say, the inconceivable power of a supernova and the miniscule power of a lightning bug. It is a totally different kind of occurrence. It is not in our power to understand how the meaning of being can be clothed in flesh, how Heaven can synchronize with Earth. We can only stand in awe before the event.

Jesus has traditionally been held to have been born without the intervention of a human father. I do not regard this as a core belief, as if a normal birth of the man Jesus would interfere with the eternal holiness of the Christ. His mother, Mary, is acknowledged to have been human since his appearance could hardly be explained otherwise. Yet some strains of Christianity have pushed the limits of Mary's humanity, making her a sinless, and certainly sexless, demigoddess whose body rose, presumably straight up, to Heaven. One is not encouraged to inquire how Heaven can be straight up from every point on a spherical earth: in Mary's day the world was flat and Heaven was a place "up there." This is not a core belief either.

Jesus did not have supernatural physical powers. He could not leap tall buildings. The miracles of the New Testament, even if they are seen as historical, do not imply a superhero so much as a man in close harmony with his Father. Jesus could not see through a brick wall but he could see through a deceptive man or woman as through window glass. That ability depends on insight, not supernatural powers.

Jesus of Nazareth was a man, species *homo sapiens*, unremarkable in appearance and chemically typical of his people. The chemistry of Jesus was mundane. He was small, dark, and probably not handsome. He had the usual complement of eyes, ears, bones, corpuscles, and chromosomes. His body was just like ours; only his soul was different. As a part of being he shared the divinity of all God's creations, all living things, and particularly all of humanity. None of that was what set him apart from us. Neither does his special divinity lie in special processes of physical genesis. He had a mother and a father of his species: our species. His mother was a teenager named Mary and his biological father was a carpenter named Joseph or some other man; we don't know and have little reason to care. Some have speculated that the biological father was a Roman centurion, possibly a rapist. It doesn't matter. Nor would it matter fundamentally if research somehow established that Jesus's name or his parents' names were not as we think we know them, or that other historical statements are inaccurate. The narrative of Jesus is news, not history.

Jesus is the incarnation of the meaning of being. His chemical composition was typical of our species. His elements have long since been dispersed. What remains – what makes him unique – is spelled out in his soul: the pattern of arrangement of the elements that composed his body. The body is gone but the pattern is eternal.

Though he was in all apparent – all chemical – ways a man like us, he was at the same time unique. God anointed him. Here is where the symbol of the virgin birth has real meaning. Paul says:

We know that the whole creation has been groaning in labor pains until now; and not only the creation, but we ourselves, who have the first fruits of the Spirit, groan inwardly while we wait for adoption, the redemption of our bodies.[62]

Mary and Joseph could produce the baby Jesus in the usual way, and since they were from all reports fine people the carpenter Jesus they reared would have been a good man. But the whole creation was not groaning for another carpenter. There is no "usual way" to introduce the meaning of being into history in the form of a man, no way for the human parents to cause or even comprehend the incarnation of the Word in their child. This was a one-time event, once in all of history. In this context we are all virgins, "the whole creation" is virginal: there is no previous earthly experience of a comparable event. Jesus as the Christ is the embodiment of the meaning of being. Jesus lived among us but lived a life unlike ours, free of estrangement from God. Wholly human, he was divine in a wholly unhuman way, as God, the author of humanity, is divine in a wholly unhuman way. As mundane as was the body of Jesus, his soul is the driving force of the New Being.

---

62 Romans 8:22-23

God and the *Other*

The appearance of Jesus as the Christ is necessary because humans have always lived in a state of estrangement from God. This predicament is not only tragic for us, it is seriously painful to God. Estrangement is the opposite of love. A few years after his visit to my college, Tillich published in the third and final volume of his "Systematic Theology"[63] a fuller answer to my question, "Why did God create us?"[64]

Remember the story about the scorpion and the bird. They make a deal: the bird will carry the scorpion across a wide river, and the scorpion won't sting him. The scorpion gets on the bird's back and the bird takes off. When they are halfway across the river the scorpion stings the bird. "What are you doing?" gasps the bird. "Now we are both going to die. Why did you sting me?"

"Because it's my nature," says the scorpion.

In effect I asked Professor Tillich, "What is the meaning of our (humans') being?" And his answer is astounding. According to Tillich, God is a principle of love. That's his nature. But love is a longing for closer union with the *other* that is the object of the love. There is such a thing as self-love. In fact it is a rare human who doesn't need to become more in touch with himself. We are estranged not only from God and each other, but from ourselves. But God is not estranged from himself. For God love is a condition that is incomplete without an *other*. Without an *other* as the object of his love it could even be said metaphorically that God is lonely. Although we are his creatures – the symbol of God the father is nowhere more apt than here – we are the *other*, the object of God's love. As blasphemous as the idea may sound, he is incomplete without us.

---

63 Tillich, Paul, *Systematic Theology*, Chicago, University of Chicago Press. *Volume 1: Reason and Revelation. Being and God.* 1951. *Volume 2: Existence and the Christ.* 1957. *Volume 3: Life and the Spirit. History and the Kingdom of God.* 1963.

64 I do not mean to suggest that Tillich's explanation was written in response to my question, which he had no doubt forgotten within hours. But it does answer my question.

This insight is electrifying because it shows that we are important, necessary, vital to God. We are at the center after all, and in a way that is not affected by the insights of Copernicus. God's creativity arises out of his love. We are not a minor chemical parlor trick in a universe created out of boredom. And we are not the worms described by some fundamentalist sects. We are sinful, we have estranged ourselves, but we are necessary to God. We are the objects of his love, created to fill that role, central to his nature. We shall see in Section 3 that this fact has a profound effect on the conditions of God's revelation of himself to us, because we must retain human freedom if we are to be fit love objects. We have human souls. We are the necessary *other* but we have estranged ourselves from God. Our estrangement is felt by God as tragic: the function of love is to conquer estrangement. That is why God paid such a heavy price to redeem us. So for us the meaning of being is love. The Sunday school maxim, "God is love" is packed with more content than one might have imagined.

The New Commandment

The great commandment Jesus taught was, "You shall love the Lord your God with all your heart, and with all your soul, and with all your strength, and with all your mind; and your neighbor as yourself."[65] The commandment of Jesus was a combination of two Old Testament commandments:

Hear, O Israel: The Lord is our God, the Lord alone. You shall love the Lord your God with all your heart, and with all your soul, and with all your might.[66]

and

You shall not hate in your heart anyone of your kin; you shall reprove your neighbor, or you will incur guilt yourself. You shall not take vengeance or bear a grudge against any of your people, but you shall love your neighbor as yourself: I am the Lord.[67]

---

65 Luke 10:27

66 Deuteronomy 6:4-5

67 Leviticus 19:17-18

It was dutifully quoted to Jesus by a lawyer seeking instruction on how to inherit eternal life.[68] There is an obvious continuity between the teachings of the Old Testament and those of the New. But the commandment of Jesus went far beyond anything made clear before his time. When the lawyer went on to ask, "Who is my neighbor?" Jesus responded with the parable of the Good Samaritan.[69] The implication was that *everyone* is a neighbor, not just members of one's family, tribe, or village. Leviticus prohibits hatred or vengeance or grudge-bearing against *anyone of your kin*; Jesus commands love for *everyone*. This understanding was an extension of Old Testament thinking but Jesus made it radical and new. John's gospel quotes him this way:

I give you a new commandment, that you love one another. **Just as I have loved you**, *you also should love one another. By this evidence everyone will know that you are my disciples, if you have love for one another.*[70] (Emphasis added)

In this form it is, as he states, a *new* commandment. "Just as I have loved you" connects the commandment to everything we know about Jesus's life, about his way of caring for the people he loved. And in the next sentence he makes this kind of love the defining evidence of discipleship. Universal obedience to this commandment would create a harmony in which God's love for all of us and ours for him and for each of our fellow humans would reinforce each other in a holy chorus.

But not one of us is ready to participate fully in the holy chorus of God's love. It remains a distant goal. God is demanding a wholehearted, soul-deep love that involves the core of our being, to answer the love that flows from God's nature itself. We do have some experience of love. When Jesus asked his disciples, "Is there anyone among you who, if your child asks for a fish, will give a snake instead

---

68 Luke 10:25-28
69 Luke 10:30-37
70 John 13:34-35

of a fish?"[71] he was pointing to one model in our experience of the love he was talking about. Humans are capable of placing a child's needs before their own, of striving continually to find ways to help the child reach his full potential. We don't all do it, and none of us does it all the time, but it's a human model we can begin to understand. Jesus embodied and commanded this kind of consuming, committed, creative love, applied not just to one's children but to everyone, always.

It's a standard we cannot reach but we need to take it seriously. It is the meaning of being.

---

71 Luke 11:11

CHAPTER 8:
The Empty Tomb

We have seen that the soul is the pattern of arrangement of all of the body's molecular components. This includes not just the DNA, which is a t_0 condition, but everything that defines the individual. The soul is conditioned by all of the individual's experiences, which are recorded by every effect of these experiences on the body. They are recorded particularly in memories. Memories are effects of experiences on part of the body: they are molecular coding in the brain. The soul is to the individual as the pattern is to the sweater. Unlike a physical entity such as a body, a pattern is indestructible: the soul is eternal.

Though our souls are eternal they are not perfect by any means. All of us are imperfect. That's why the incarnation was needed. Our inability to love fully – to participate in the holy chorus of perfect human and divine love described in Chapter 7 – is our estrangement from God. It results in what are called sinful acts and sins of inaction, but the fundamental problem is sin itself: estrangement, separation. Sin is the gap we cannot bridge between existence as we experience it and what we were created to be. Since we cannot be as we are meant to be, God miraculously clothed the meaning of being in human flesh. Jesus as the Christ shows us the meaning of being and reconciles us to God.

Jesus, the anointed of God, entered history to be crucified in order to redeem us. He manifested God's love, he taught us the way, he showed us how to live, he told us what we needed to hear. Then he accepted torture and death as an essential part of his mission. God's love can be expressed in ways that seem harsh to humans, as set out most compellingly in the book of Job. The brief life and shocking death of Jesus showed that God was committed to his children in the most serious way. By word and example, Jesus showed the life humans were to strive for. When he laid down his life he demonstrated that he shared every human experience: that God and man were at one. It is crucial to the narrative that Jesus did not accept martyrdom comfortably, with godlike serenity. In the Garden of Gethsemane his sweat was like blood as he asked to be excused; on the cross he screamed in pain and demanded to know why God had abandoned him. He suffered everything a human can suffer except estrangement from God, and the suffering was real, intense, horrible. It is not that appeasement of God required a human sacrifice like the animal sacrifices prescribed in the Old Testament. Rather, God made the greatest of all sacrifices to appease *us*, delivering his own anointed one to crucifixion, showing that he withheld nothing, setting the stage for a new life in his followers to the present day and beyond.

God showed that though we are not acceptable he accepts us.

The Resurrection Message

The narrative doesn't end there, of course. Some would say that's where it begins. Two days after his crucifixion the women closest to Jesus go to his tomb. It is Sunday morning, about forty hours after the Friday afternoon when he was murdered, and they are there to carry out the sad ceremonies surrounding death in their tradition. They enter the tomb but they don't carry out any sad ceremonies. Instead they are granted the galvanizing insight of the age. In Luke's description, two men in dazzling clothes ask them:

Why do you look for the living among the dead? He is not here, but has risen.[72]

That is the core of the Easter narrative. The meaning of being, the women discovered for all of us, was not to be sought among the dead but among the living. The tomb could not hold him. His followers had lived with him, listened to him, watched him, betrayed him, denied him, given up on him, breathed him. Now he was part of them, living within them. His soul had become an integral part

---

72 Luke 24:5

of theirs – and ours. His DNA was not physically transferred like a virus invading a body. Rather, he entered into his disciples, and through them eventually into us, on the basis of his manifestation and message. There was no escape: he lived in them and in those who came after.

We don't have to focus on the question of whether Jesus physically rose from the dead in his original body. The essential requirement was that the Word, the meaning, be transmitted to humankind. For the murdered Carpenter to reappear bodily two thousand years ago, to walk the sands of Palestine for a month and a half, would beyond question be a demonstration of great power. I am not arguing that such a demonstration would be impossible for God. But a greater demonstration was made in the creation of the universe; God had no need to show his power in so miniscule a matter as the physical resuscitation of the Carpenter. A bodily reappearance would mark Jesus as unique but his uniqueness is manifest much more in the life he lived and in his living presence today.

Everything about the history of those events two thousand years ago is subject to doubt. The gospels are not reliable history. They were not written by eyewitnesses and the earliest, Mark, was written at least twenty years after the death of Jesus and perhaps much later. The writers all had individual viewpoints and were affected by different political pressures and events; each had a unique perspective and a specific purpose in writing. It is not going too far to say that each had an ax to grind. Yet whatever the truth about the resurrection then, to be a modern Christian is to be directly conscious of the living presence of Christ today. Science has no rebuttal to this consciousness.

Christians hold that Jesus was imprinted on his followers, living as a spirit within them and continuing alive to this day and beyond. That is the resurrection that has real significance. If one had a choice of one and only one of the possible meanings of the resurrection, which would have practical importance today? If the crucified Carpenter reappeared briefly in Palestine and then had no further influence on mankind, his resurrection would be an amazing event with little real impact upon our lives. It would probably be forgotten by now. But whether or not the Carpenter walked after Good Friday, the presence of Christ within us changes the conditions of being for us fundamentally and forever: "Everything old has passed away; see, everything has become new!"

Here is the message of the empty tomb: Jesus's meaning to our being has survived his brief time on Earth. *That's* the miracle. There was no need for deeds of power. Somehow the manifestation of the meaning of being took root in humankind. When Jesus says, "No one comes to the Father except through me,"[73] he is stating that only God can heal the estrangement caused by mankind's sinful nature, not that only members of the Christian churches can have an eternal relationship with God. With his coming Christ inaugurates the New Being, reconciliation with God, acceptance in the face of our unacceptability.

Uploading the Soul

As this acceptance does not end with the death of Jesus, there is no evidence that it must end with ours. There are many who believe that survival of a personality after death is impossible. They consider Jesus's promise of eternal life absurd because within a few years of a person's death nothing appears to survive. "You are dust, and to dust you shall return"[74] we are told, correctly but incompletely. Henry Wadsworth Longfellow commented,

> *Dust thou art, to dust returnest,*
> *Was not spoken of the soul.*

Our hardware is indeed the dust of the earth. But the defining essence of a living being is not the elemental dust of which he is built but the pattern, the blueprint, the software that describes how the elements are arranged: in short, the soul. As the values in the decimal places of π are indestructible, a software pattern is indestructible and certainly is not limited to the hardware it once animated. The soul is immortal.

---

73 John 14:6
74 Genesis 3:19

Software is easily transmitted from point to point, electronically. Programs can be downloaded to a computer from the Internet, and can be uploaded just as easily. The information travels at nearly the speed of light. A program can be shared with a colleague in China in virtually no time. But software is in essence a pattern that does not depend on the elements arranged. The pattern that defined Mother Theresa as she was at a particular time could in principle be incorporated into a very long e-mail message, and the soul of Mother Theresa could travel at the speed of light, to animate a new body.

This model tells us that the continued existence of a personality with all its memories, hopes, and fears, is not impossible. And it does not require the continued association of the physical elements that constituted its body. All that is required for the continuing existence of an individual personality after the body is gone is for the software – the soul – to be uploaded. Immortality can not be proven by the methods of science but it is not inconsistent with any scientific finding.

How is this uploading accomplished? To where is the soul uploaded? To animate what sort of body? The answers are not available in this life. We do know the reason for the uploading: because we are the objects of God's love. For answers to the other questions, we will have to wait.

SECTION 3:
The Breath of Being

We believe in the Holy Spirit, the Lord, the giver of life, who proceeds from the Father and the Son. With the Father and the Son he is worshipped and glorified. He has spoken through the Prophets. We believe in one holy catholic and apostolic Church. We acknowledge one baptism for the forgiveness of sins. We look for the resurrection of the dead, and the life of the world to come.

Amen.

CHAPTER 9:
Inspiration and Revelation

While we wait for the answers we hope to get in a future sphere of being, we can ponder our living response today to the gifts we have been given. The Father has created us; the Son has redeemed us. The third person of the trinity has a continuing role: inspiration.

In German, the word *spirit* is translated *geist*. *Zeitgeist*, for example, means the spirit of the time. The traditional term in English, Holy Ghost, is related to *geist*. In some contexts *geistlich* can be rendered *ghostly*, in others *spiritual*. When I learned the Creed we recited, "We believe in the Holy Ghost..." But since the concept involved bears little resemblance to Halloween spooks, the term Holy Spirit makes more sense to modern ears. The Latin *spiro* means *I breathe*: spirit and breath are one. When we are inspired we inhale the Holy Spirit: the holy breath of God enters us. When we expire – the archaic term is *give up the ghost* – we breathe our last and the Spirit leaves our body. The harpsichord at the St. Paul Chamber Orchestra bears, in Latin, the inscription, "Let everything that breathes praise the Lord," which is the climax of Psalm 150. Unable to recall the source of this passage, I spent some time trying to translate it using my weak high school Latin. I thought it might either mean "All my spirit, praise the Lord," or "All that breathes, praise the Lord." I was right to hesitate between these renderings as they are closely related. The Gospel of John reports that when the risen Jesus appeared to his disciples, "...he breathed on them and said to them, 'Receive the Holy Spirit.' " [75]

In Santa Fe we have spectacular sunsets. Our Golden Retriever, Toby, has never shown the slightest interest in one. It may be that

---

75 John 20:22

dogs are color blind; the research on this point is inconsistent. In any case they are not interested in sunsets or in beautiful paintings. But if the wind blows when Toby is out for a walk, he perks up and turns to face directly into it. It's hard to get him to move on. Wind … breath… spirit... They are all related to the same Latin and Greek roots. We humans can detect only a fraction of what Toby is sniffing. While dogs may be colorblind, their sense of smell is a hundred times more acute than ours. No one watching Toby can doubt that the wind carries messages for dogs. The wind is Earth's breath. The Holy Spirit is God's breath. As Toby faces into the wind and receives its messages, he reminds us to open ourselves to the messages of the Holy Spirit.

Spirit and Ether

It is easy to form some image of God the Father: he is the creator of all that is. God the Son we understand as our reconciler. We know what a father is, and a son. God the Holy Spirit is a less vivid image, even though the Spirit is today our direct contact with God. God the creator is the ground of being, and God the son is the meaning of being. The Holy Spirit is the breath of being: God communicating with us, filling us, inspiring us.[76] And as the Father is the ground of being and the Son is the ground of meaning, the Spirit is the ground of revelation.

The Gospel of John reports this promise from Jesus to his disciples:

If you love me, you will keep my commandments. And I will ask the Father, and he will give you another Advocate, to be with you forever. This is the Spirit of truth, whom the world cannot receive, because it neither sees him or knows him. You know him, because he abides with you, and he will be in you.[77]

Here's another way to think about the Holy Spirit. In the late Nineteenth Century transmission of light and other electromagnetic waves was believed to take place through the medium of the

76   Here the medical and religious uses of *inspire* part company. A physician would say that when we breathe air is inspired. But when we take in the Holy Spirit it is we who are inspired.

77   John 14:15-17

luminiferous ether. Everything moved through the ether, which provided a fixed reference for all motion including that of light. Light was a sort of vibration in the ether, analogous to sound waves moving through a tangible medium like air, or water, or steel. Sound cannot be transmitted through vacuum but light can. The reason was believed to be that light traveled through the ether, which permeated all space including vacuum. One could say that the ether was the ground, the medium, of light. In the same way, the Holy Spirit – the Spirit of truth – is the ground of revelation, the medium through which God offers his light, his presence, to humanity. By the way, a crucial experiment by Albert Michelson and Edward Morley in 1887 raised questions about the luminiferous ether. Eighteen years later Einstein's interpretation of that experiment blew away belief in the ether and introduced the Special Theory of Relativity. The Holy Spirit was unaffected.

Our perception of the divine requires that the divine be willing to be perceived. God is radically unlike us, even though we are created in his image. If he chose to be inscrutable we would have no way of knowing him even in the dim way we do. We cannot reason our way to God. What we know of God is what he reveals to us. Revelation is a function of the Holy Spirit operating in a variety of ways. Scriptures have revealed God to mankind progressively over the centuries. A single once and for all revelation would not do because while God is the same yesterday, today, and forever, humankind is not. A crucial feature of revelation is that it depends not only on the source but on the recipient.

The Revelation of the Khrrreegmzzhians

To understand why this is so, consider a science fiction scenario. Let's imagine that the Grrragnaall family from the planet Khrrreegmzzh (these names are pronounced just as they're spelled – in Khrrreegmzzhese) in a far-off galaxy visited Earth ten thousand years ago. The people of Khrrreegmzzh were already far more advanced than we are even now. Now I present for your consideration young Hjrrlndr "Bunny" Grrragnaall, a brilliant but immature teenager. Khrrreegmzzhian years are much longer than Earth's so Bunny was actually over sixty of our years old, but she was still a student. Bunny was required to bring along on vacation her text book on simple introductory mathematical physics. It seems she had been goofing off in school: she flunked her examination on fundamentals of time travel. The book, though at a beginning level by the standards of Khrrreegmzzh, consisted almost entirely of long multidimensional equations. Using a classic teenager's strategy, Bunny contrived to "lose" the text book by burying it in a swamp, putting an end to tiresome assignments. After a pleasant holiday the Grrragnaall family returned home. Bunny eventually got her degree and the Grrragnaalls lived happily ever after, so far as we know.

Five thousand years later geophysical forces bring the buried book to the surface, where it is found by local tribesmen, possibly ancestors of Moses. The book contains, among other marvels, the secrets of antigravity and time travel, which are elementary stuff for Khrrreegmzzhese. The tribesmen pass the book around and pretend to examine it while stroking their beards and looking wise. Finally, after discovering that they can't possibly understand a word by reading it, they take it in by the only means available to them: they eat the book. It doesn't taste good and does not improve their understanding, but they can make no other use of this treasure, because the meaning of a mathematical equation becomes apparent only when the reader, on his own, has worked through mathematics up to that point. You can't start with the mathematics of time travel (assuming there is any such thing.) The tribesmen are not ready for the profundities of the book from Khrrreegmzzh. The revelation has been uncovered but not received. The entire incident is forgotten.

There is a point to this foolishness: revelation that cannot be received by humans at a particular stage of development is only *potential* revelation. The information is uncovered but the message cannot be read. The situation is precisely analogous to that of the tribesmen with the book on time travel. And so what we know of God's will for us can be seen to evolve over time, not because God's message fundamentally evolves but because humankind's ability to understand does:

I still have many things to say to you, but you cannot bear them now. When the Spirit of truth comes, he will guide you into all the truth...[78]

The first chapter of Genesis describes the creation of the universe. As a human parent parcels out information to a small child in comprehensible portions – computer folk call these portions bytes – so revelation comes to adults in portions for which they are ready. It would make no more sense to speak of intergalactic dust to people three thousand years ago than to describe the subtleties of human sexuality to a six-year-old today. People three millennia ago would not have been edified by a description of the Big Bang, coalescence of interstellar material into galaxies and stars, exploding supernovas, cooling planets, and the machinery sketched in Section 1 that led to the appearance of our species. They could not have chewed those bytes. It was enough to understand through the mythic story that the earth, the heavens, all that we are, and all that we have are God's gift. This understanding is in no way contradicted by the results of modern cosmology.

Some religious authorities are horrified by the modern cosmological understanding but others, including some who are by no means theologically liberal, are quite comfortable with it:

The Bible itself speaks to us of the origin of the universe and its make-up, not in order to provide us with a scientific treatise but in order to state the correct relationships of man with God and with the universe. Sacred scripture wishes simply to declare that the world was created by God, and in order to teach this truth it expresses itself in the terms of the cosmology in use at the time of the writer...[The Bible] does not wish to teach us how the heavens were made but how one goes to Heaven.

The speaker was the late Pope John Paul II, addressing the pontifical Academy of Sciences in 1981, the same year that Steven Hawking discussed cosmology at the Vatican.

Angels, Sock Puppets, and Stenographers

We can imagine God creating beings who, right from the start, could understand his message in its entirety. Maybe angels are like

---

[78] John 16:12-13

that. The trouble is that such creatures could only be pale imitations of God. Angels, if they exist at all, are boring. They carry God's messages but they add or subtract nothing and their behavior is predictable. A lonely child can insert his hand into a sock to create a simple puppet. He can manipulate his fingers inside the sock and learn to create an effect that looks something like a mouth, so he can have conversations with his puppet. He obviously knows that he is carrying on both ends of the conversation but if he has no one better to talk with he can talk with his sock puppet. If someone more rewarding comes along – a parent, a teacher, a schoolmate, even a younger child – he abandons the sock puppet because he prefers to converse with someone other than himself. Angels are sock puppets, but we are not. We are created in the image of God, but we are not imitation Gods. God's love requires objects *other* than himself. This is the role he created us for. We are beings of our own sort. That's what qualifies us to be the recipients of revelation, even though our understanding progresses with agonizing slowness. Like the recipients of the Khrrreegmzzhian book, we cannot take in God's teaching without working our way through to understanding. This process is of course far from complete.

God's need for an *other* as the object of his love requires that his revelation be delivered to creatures no less autonomous than human beings. Otherwise he would, in effect, be revealing himself to himself: conversing with a sock puppet. Impressive as earth's non-human creatures are, they do not have independent minds capable of pondering spiritual and moral issues. They are thus in large measure automatons. But human beings are not automatons and God does not mold us by brute force, even though it would be quicker. To do so would be to destroy the independence that makes us eligible to be the objects of his love. Instead he allows us to develop slowly and hesitantly under his patient guidance. God is not in a hurry. He does not thrust his revelation upon us. The Spirit is a breath, not a typhoon. And so scripture is not a stenographic record of words the Holy Spirit roared into the ears of passive scribes. Rather, active individuals breathed in the Holy Spirit and were inspired to share their growing understanding.

They were people of their times, reverently trying to make sense of God's will. In this way they were like us. Some recounted bits of history as they knew it, some wove myths, some wrote essays and poems and prophecies. Taken as a whole their work is inspired by God and reveals God's truth, the Word. The Bible is a magnificent record of the way people limited to their own times came progressively to understand God's revelation.

But scripture is not dictated word by word to stenographers: *"Yes, Mr. Yahweh, I have all that up to 'adulthood'. Or was it 'adultery?' "*

That's not how the Bible is inspired. It would be absurd to extract a verse here and a verse there out of context and understand the result, literally and uncritically, as a divine commandment for living in today's world. Times have changed and we have learned a thing or two in the last two millennia. Genesis describes the sky as a dome that "separated the waters that were under the dome from the waters that were above the dome."[79] It is a beautiful image. The Church in Galileo's time wanted to continue to paint the stars and planets literally on the dome, and was prepared to use its muscle against anyone who suggested a contradictory picture. The Church missed the point of Genesis and made itself ridiculous long before space probes penetrated the dome.

God is not the God of the Deists, who taught that he created the universe and then left it on its own. Neither is he the God of the literalists, who understand as historical such accounts as the sun stopping in the sky at Joshua's command, a function of the direct intervention of God. Rather than as a creator who lost interest in his creation or a flamboyant magician who at every instant shows his contempt for his own natural laws, God nudges the course of human history today through the creative whispers of the Holy Spirit. The course of history is changed when humans act in response to these whispers.

The ultimate revelation is the fact of Jesus as the Christ, the incarnation of the meaning of being. But even though Christ is the final revelation, our understanding is not final. Theologians are not made redundant by the fact of a final revelation, because mankind's reception of this revelation continues to evolve.

---

79 Genesis 1: 7

CHAPTER 10:
The Media of Revelation

The evolving growth in our reception of revelation is a function of the Holy Spirit working in our minds and hearts. Though the Spirit is conceptually less tangible than the creator-father or the redeemer-son, it is the Spirit who touches us directly. Few if any face-to-face encounters with the Father or the Son have been reliably reported in the last two millennia, but the Spirit, though not visible, is available to us on a daily basis. As the Spirit is subtle, encounters with the Spirit are subtle. Yet they are the media through which God works in the world, through which he communicates with his creatures today.

Marshall McLuhan described a medium as an extension of ourselves.[80] In Lutheran catechism classes, we used the term, *means of grace*, to describe God's media. I was required to memorize them: scripture, baptism, and communion, or in the language of the Catechism, "the Word of God, the Sacrament of Holy Baptism, and the Sacrament of the Altar." To this I would add prayer. These are the media through which God works in us, the media of revelation. In Chapter 11 we'll talk about scripture: communication through the medium of the written word. The other three media are discussed here.

Prayer

The satirist Ambrose Bierce wrote that to pray is "to ask that the laws of the universe be annulled in behalf of a single petitioner confessedly unworthy." There are people who pray in this way, like

---

80 McLuhan, Marshall, *Understanding Media: The Extensions of Man*, New York, The McGraw-Hill Book Company, 1964

faxing a lunch order to a restaurant, expecting miracles on demand. They are appalled if they receive dry cheese on stale bread. But prayer does not exist in order for us to instruct God about what he needs to attend to. We are the ones who need instruction. The Lord's Prayer does contain one clause that is, in form, a request for a tangible benefit. But "Give us this day our daily bread" is not, for most of us, a plea for enough food to allow us to get through the day. Instead it's a recollection and a celebration of the source of all that we have, in the spirit of the Jewish prayer of praise to the Lord who brings out bread from the ground. If we really are hungry we'd better get to work; prayer by itself will not provide food for our bodies.

Over the years, there have been experiments attempting to test whether prayer actually has objective effects. For example, volunteers have been asked to pray for good results for patients undergoing critical medical procedures. The devout Christians doing the praying didn't know the patients; they were told only the first name and diagnosis. A number of factors can destroy the credibility of such an experiment, and results were variable. After successively better experimental designs substantially reduced the effect of such factors there was little or no robust evidence of the efficacy of prayer. But in considering these experiments it's hard to see that prayer as we understand it was really studied. Participants recited a formula naming someone with whom they had no relationship at all. It's as if I were to pick a name at random from the phone book and "pray" for good luck for that person. Such a procedure would not improve his chance of winning the lottery. I don't think that's prayer and I would be astonished if God found it a useful basis for his decisions. I don't think these experiments, however refined they may be in the future, will tell us anything about the efficacy of prayer.

Rather than a faxed-in lunch order, prayer is a conversation in which we try to get in touch with the eternal. We ponder issues and concerns under the guidance of the Holy Spirit. Through the medium of the Spirit we are extended to try to feel the mind of God. When we pray for someone who is sick we remember the need of the patient and his family members for comfort, we remind them of God's love, we are reminded of our own responsibilities, we express our love and support, we recall the miracles of treatment God has made available. We do not need to remind God of anything and we need not expect *his* behavior to be modified by our advice. The act of prayer changes things because it changes *us*.

I don't mean that nothing tangible results from prayer. The patient is aware that his friends are praying for him. He is lifted, supported, comforted. He feels the breath that is the Holy Spirit. Those offering the prayers think more deeply about ~~the~~ his needs and are moved to offer personal support and assistance. His family members are also supported and are more able to attend to him. For all of these reasons recovery is hastened. A sick person who is confident and relaxed is much more likely to get well: any doctor, regardless of his views on the Holy Spirit, will agree that a positive state of mind improves the patient's chances. This is an observed fact, recognized since ancient times, though the biochemical reasons are not yet clear. In the healing stories of the New Testament Jesus often tells the people who have been healed, "*Your faith* has made you well."[81]

Yet the meaning of healing is not restricted to recovery from illness. The person who is optimistic yet reconciled to his fate, who is at peace with God and his neighbors, has been healed whether he lives or dies. When we pray for healing for ourselves or others we need to leave the nature of the healing to God. No one leaves this world alive and God does not occupy himself eliminating tumors and arterial blockages. To pray for recovery rather than for healing raises troubling questions. We know, for example, that not everyone with cancer is cured. If it is God who rules that one person must live and one must die, how does he decide which is the lucky survivor? If it is on the basis of intercessory prayer, is it God's practice to preserve the one who has the greatest number of devout friends? How would we explain to the widow that God loved her late husband less than he loved the survivor? If God were active in curing fatal diseases, would he not know before hearing from us which patients "should"

---

81 Luke 17:19 among others

be cured and which allowed to die? Why would he change his mind on the basis of our meager wisdom? Of course we will pray for recovery when our loved ones are in mortal danger and it is understandable that we should express our longing in this way. And if recovery follows it is right that we should express our relief and gratitude, even though God already knows. God is the author of all forms of healing and modern medicine is one of the tools of his grace. But it is a distortion to pray over a patient with a blocked coronary artery and to feel betrayed if the X-ray fails to show the blockage obediently dissolving as a result of our pleas.

And when we pray for rain we should not expect God to push clouds around against the wind. The prayer for rain focuses our attention on the source of all the amenities that make life possible, on the mercy of God that makes a home for us in the universe. We contemplate ourselves in our role as stewards of the biosphere sustained by rain. We share our pain at the deprivations resulting from drought and are comforted and strengthened for the arid path we are treading. And when rain comes, as in our experience it always has, we remember its ultimate source. If, as now seems possible, our flawed stewardship of the planet results in its becoming hostile to our species, we will only be able to gasp out our final prayer for forgiveness.

Prayer is a two-way conversation with God, made possible by the Holy Spirit acting within us. Saint Paul points out that we do not know how to pray as we ought, but that the Spirit helps us in our weakness, interceding with "sighs too deep for words."[82] This experience does not change God but it changes us. A child's "God bless Mommy and Daddy and Fido" takes the child out of himself and gives him a glimpse of others with needs. The child cannot fill these needs but he can start to appreciate them. This begins the process by which he may come to some sense of a power that cares for him and for all of us. Prayer does the same thing for adults: from God's perspective an adult's understanding is at best little different from a child's:

---

82 Romans 8:26

"Truly I tell you, whoever does not receive the kingdom of God as a little child will never enter it."[83]

And if prayer changes us, makes us more receptive to the Spirit, then God may be able to make use of our changed selves to give a new answer to the prayer.

Eucharist

God's grace is also revealed through sacraments, of which the most important – in many denominations the only ones – are baptism and communion or Eucharist. In Eucharist the communicant ingests small samples of consecrated bread and wine and in some way receives the gift of Christ through the action of the Holy Spirit. This is a mystery, not to be fully comprehended in human terms but partially understood in a variety of ways. The Roman Catholic church teaches that when the elements – the bread and wine – are consecrated, they are wholly changed. Despite appearances, that which essentially makes bread bread and wine wine has been replaced: it is gone. After consecration, also known as the elevation of the host, neither bread nor wine is present; only the true body and blood of Christ remain, and it is these that are consumed. In the Latin mass, *"hoc est corpus"* – "this is the body" – means that the body of Christ is physically present, *replacing* the bread that has been transformed. It seems natural that *"hoc est corpus"* has been corrupted into the magician's "hocus pocus" for magical appearances, disappearances, and transformations.

The Lutheran church, on the other hand, denies that the bread and wine disappear. The essence of bread and wine are still present, but so is the essence of the body and blood of Christ. Lutheran doctrine asserts that the body and blood are physically present "in, with, and under" the consecrated bread and wine. I was well schooled as a Lutheran candidate for confirmation, but neither I nor anyone else can tell you what "in, with, and under" means. It is understood to be a mystery. What I can tell you is that Lutherans insist they

---

83 Mark 10:17

believe in the physical presence of body and blood as truly as do Roman Catholics, but that after consecration *all four* substances are essentially present: bread, wine, body, and blood. The difference is more theoretical than practical or sensible – the wine's bouquet is not lost, nor is it improved, when it is consecrated – but it seems to be important to some Roman Catholics and Lutherans.

Most Protestant denominations reject equally the Roman Catholic transubstantiation and the Lutheran consubstantiation and teach that the bread and wine remain bread and wine. At the same time, the Eucharist is a key sacrament, and the body and blood of Christ are considered to be truly present. The shades of distinction among these views are far more apparent than real, even though they have on occasion been considered vitally and even mortally important. Lutherans, Roman Catholics, and all denominations agree that the materials consumed have all the superficial properties of bread and wine. The bread will nourish: its calorie count is unchanged. The wine will intoxicate: churches sometimes have to secure their sacramental supplies against theft by miscreants whose thirst is apparently more for alcohol than for the blood of Christ. The Roman Catholic insists that the bread and wine are no longer essentially present after consecration, while acknowledging that what is present is in all objective ways just like bread and wine. The Lutheran considers that the bread and wine are still present, but that body and blood are also truly present though they can in no way be detected. It is hard to see how one would act or think or feel differently on the basis of this distinction.

George Herbert makes the point elegantly in his poem, "The Holy Communion", which reads, in part:

ffirst I am sure, whether bread stay
Or whether Bread doe fly away
Concerneth bread, not mee.
But that both thou and all thy traine
Bee there, to thy truth, and my gaine,
Concerneth mee and Thee.

Herbert is emphasizing that there is substance, without regard to the details of theology, to the statement that the body and blood of Christ are truly present.

The Gospel of John quotes Jesus as saying:

"Those who eat my flesh and drink my blood have eternal life, and I will raise them up on the last day; for my flesh is true food and my blood is true drink. Those who eat my flesh and drink my blood abide in me, and I in them. Just as the living Father sent me, and I live because of the Father, so whoever eats me will live because of me. This is the bread that came down from heaven, not like that which your ancestors ate, and they died. But the one who eats this bread will live forever."[84]

Robert Heinlein's novel, *Stranger in a Strange Land*, tells the story of a baby born on Mars of parents who were explorers from Earth. Something of a Christ figure, the grown man is taken to the strange land: Earth. He finds our ways unfathomable, and struggles to understand. The Martian word for the profound understanding he seeks is *"grok."* The Earthlings who encounter him are surprised to learn that the literal translation of *"grok"* is *"drink."* In a similar spirit, when we eat and drink Christ we take him in, we incorporate him into ourselves. To the extent we are able, we *grok* him.

The body and blood have special meaning for Christians. Christ's body is the incarnation of the meaning of being. The sudden appearance two thousand years ago of the incarnate Word is the central event of history. The blood of Christ, shed willingly on the cross, is the sacrifice showing that God withheld nothing in redeeming us. In this sense, the bread is Christmas and the wine is Good Friday, the gateway to Easter. The consumption of these elements is not an act of physical or symbolic cannibalism. It is a commemoration of the twin towers of our faith. The consecrated bread and wine are powerful symbols of the sacrifices made to institute the New Being for us. They appeal directly to our senses over the heads of our conscious thoughts. The feel of the bread, the bouquet and taste of the wine, even the sound made when the bread is broken, put us

---

84 John 6:54-58

in touch with the hundreds of times we have been here before, with the last supper itself, two millennia in the past, with the agony of Golgotha. The elevation of the host occurs when the communicant receives the bread and wine and by the power of the Holy Spirit perceives in a new way the living presence of Christ.

Baptism

The Creed says we believe in baptism for the forgiveness of sins. This was traditionally interpreted as relating to original sin, and many Roman Catholics once believed that babies who die unbaptised cannot enter into God's presence. Actually, while this was taught in Roman Catholic catechisms, it was never fully accepted Church doctrine and I'm happy to report that it has now been abandoned. Similarly, three generations ago, the Lutheran liturgy included words to approximately (I quote from memory) this effect: "We know that babies, while seemingly innocent, are in reality full of sin…" This strange notion doesn't receive the emphasis it once did, and the statement is gone from more recent versions of the liturgy. Original sin, in the sense of sin-filled infants, appears to be on the way out in many places. Good riddance.

Yet the Credal description of baptism stands. Sin is separation from God, the separation to which we are all subject, even from birth. It is not that babies commit sinful acts but that we all have the *propensity* to commit these acts. The symbol of Adam's fall, making Christ's sacrifice necessary, emphasizes our helplessness to achieve reconciliation on our own. That's not because God refuses to reconcile; he is eager for us at any time. But we are not equipped to come to him, even though he is always present wherever we are. And it's hard for us to open ourselves so that he can come to us. Baptism represents a ceremonial entrance into God's church, the fellowship of believers. Thus while it has roots in ancient purification rites, baptism takes a new meaning for Christians. The water of baptism symbolizes a new birth into the fellowship. It is within the church that most Christians are reconciled with God. That's what forgiveness of sin means. The Holy Spirit is breathed in by individuals, but Christianity is not best practiced in isolation. Protestant sects have little tradition of cloistered monks, much less of holy hermits. No Christian is intended to be a solo practitioner.

Important commitments are undertaken by the baptismal candidate and by sponsors. The candidate renounces sin and accepts Christ as savior, teacher, and exemplar. Baptism is a communal sacrament because the new member is welcomed by the congregants present, who share in his commitments. More often than not baptism is administered to infants; entrance into the fellowship of believers is regarded as the place to start a life of discipleship. The sponsors take the commitment on behalf of the young candidate and commit themselves to make sure the candidate is reared in the Christian life and faith. The candidate will have opportunities when sufficiently mature to reaffirm the commitment for himself. So the sacrament is important to the entire community: the sponsors are inspired to rear the candidate as a follower of Christ; the candidate enters the fellowship; the congregation receives a new member whom it is committed to guide and support and from whom it expects a life of Christian service.

Jesus gathered disciples and, having taught them, sent them into the world to proclaim the good news:

"Go therefore and make disciples of all nations, baptizing them in the name of the Father and of the Son and of the Holy Spirit, and teaching them to obey everything that I have commanded you. And remember, I am with you always, to the end of the age." [85]

The apostles continued his work after his death and resurrection, as the followers of Jesus became a powerful force, first within Judaism and very soon independently. The church of Christ became a mass movement. The Creed speaks of "one holy catholic and apostolic Church." It always considered itself holy because it was founded to proclaim the good news of God's anointed one. It came to speak of itself as catholic – that is, universal – because the good news was for "all nations": for everyone. And it regards itself as apostolic

---

85 Matthew 28:19-20

because it is the current day's recipient of Jesus's injunction to "go and make disciples"; the church's members are the modern apostles, the executors of the legacy of Jesus.

The Imperfect Church

The visible church – the church as humans experience and participate in it – is a human approximation of God's holy fellowship. Because it is human it is far from perfect. Over centuries this powerful institution has been a civilizing influence, organizing great works of charity, art, education, and mercy. It has also been responsible for great barbarity: wars of conquest, forced conversions, inquisitions, torture. Today people look at some of the things churches do and wonder how a just and loving God could be imagined behind what is seen. One sect enables its officials to commit unspeakable crimes against children. Another decides to fracture over narrow questions of personal morality and begins spending its time in lawsuits over real estate. Still another forces female children into plural marriages with elderly men. The church is people, and that means it is sometimes people doing reprehensible things. Yet it remains the image of God's fellowship. It needs to be criticized, but more importantly it needs to be improved from within. Giving up is not a useful option.

Nor is division cause for despair. The church began in schism, as Christianity separated itself from Judaism. It has since been severed by a succession of schisms, first in the separation of the Eastern Orthodox rites from those of Roman Catholicism and later by the centrifugal forces of the Protestant Reformation, protesting against all that diminished or distorted the church. There are now scores of Christian sects, each of which is a human representation of the one holy catholic and apostolic church and each of which contains its own human distortions. This separation is not in itself tragic, though many tragic acts have resulted from attempts to heal schism by force. If there were only a single sect it would still be an earthly representation of God's fellowship and it would not remain free from error. The Roman Catholic church in its time of dominance made errors; the affair of Galileo was not the first or the last time it insisted on things it now renounces. All of us as humans continue, in Paul's term, to grope for God. Now that no one sect is dominant, a free exchange of ideas is one route to a closer approximation to the truth.

The churches today proclaim the good news and at the same time show the meaning of a human response to God's mercy through good works. For any one of them to claim sole proprietorship of the truth, or exclusive commission from God, is hubris. Whenever a church has placed its institutional prestige at the top of its list of priorities it has risked catastrophe, as happened in the cover-up of the child abuse scandal within the Roman Catholic church. But when the churches put aside their claims to exclusive knowledge of the truth, abandon useless arguments about inessentials, and stand together for what is essential, they approach more closely the true church of God.

CHAPTER 11:
The Moral Content of Revelation

I argued in Chapter 9 that human understanding of God's revelation is continuing to evolve. This evolving understanding clearly extends to moral issues; in fact moral issues are right at its center. Much of the law of the Old Testament is contained in the book of Leviticus. Among other injunctions Leviticus thunders, "You shall not lie with a male as with a woman; it is an abomination."[86] But before concluding that this amounts to a literal and infallible guide to our behavior today, we should understand something about the context. To the author of Leviticus, homosexual sex was, in fact, an abomination committed by followers of a competing god. That's what made it so abominable.

I have some experience with the kind of rage expressed in Leviticus. I grew up in Queens, New York, which is adjacent to Brooklyn. Yankee Stadium is in the Bronx, farther from Queens. My parents and I were Yankee fans while most of the big kids on our block were fans of the Brooklyn Dodgers. The problem with big kids is that they're...big. They tend to win fights with littler kids and I generally lost in my conflicts with the Dodger fans I grew up with. To this day I am not fond of the Dodgers and I am not mollified by their move to Los Angeles half a century ago. Like the boy objecting to broccoli in a New Yorker cartoon, I say they're still the Brooklyn Dodgers and I say the hell with them. That's pretty much the attitude of Yahweh's people toward the followers of their competing god. Adult competitions about their gods are as intense as kids' competitions about their baseball teams, and sometimes more so. Kids don't commit genocide over baseball.

---

86 Leviticus 18:22

I still root for any other team to beat the Dodgers: "You shall not lose to the Dodgers; they are an abomination!" But my infantile rejection of this team has no adult basis today. Similarly, the rage of Leviticus is not a sufficient basis for deciding contemporary moral questions. It leaves out the new insights of Jesus as well as ongoing discussion and debate on these serious topics. We need to give more consideration to the evolution of our understanding over the millennia. For this purpose it will be helpful to bring our sketch of earliest prehistory further forward, in order to link up today's understanding with what has gone before.

The Timeline of the Universe

We have seen that the universe is about 13.7 billion years old. Of course that figure is not exact: formally it could mean anything from 13.65 billion to 13.75 billion, and even at this modest level of precision ($\pm$ fifty million years) it is not guaranteed to be accurate. But as an exercise suppose that t_0 is *exactly* 13,700,000,000 (thirteen billion, seven hundred million) years ago. The resulting timeline might look something like Table 1. Galaxies start to form around a million years after the big bang and within them stars form.[87] Planet Earth begins to coalesce at time t=9.1 billion (that is, 9.1 billion years after t_0, or 4.6 billion years before the present), and cools by t=9.7 billion. The self-replicating molecules we spoke of in Chapter 5 appear, perhaps, around t=10.9 billion; nobody is too sure since the earliest life forms left no fossil traces that we know of. Fossil traces of organisms dating to 2.8 billion years ago – that is, t=10.9 billion – have been reported. Fossils from more evolved life forms become much more abundant around t=13.156 billion.

It is interesting to note this gap of over two billion years between when we guess life began and the time period for which fossil evidence is abundant. Intelligent design advocates are fond of challenging their opponents to produce life from a jar of chemicals by some random process. They fail to note that it is difficult, or at least

---

87 Hawking, Steven and Mlodinow, Leonard, *A Briefer History of Time*, New York, Bantam Dell, 2005

time-consuming, to replicate an experiment that went on for as much as three billion years with constantly changing conditions. No one suggests that a jar of chemicals will produce Mozart within the span of a research grant. I don't know whether it will happen in some of our lifetimes, but certainly before we have waited a millionth of three billion years life will be created in the lab from jars of chemicals. Of course that's only a first step toward producing a mammal, much less a human, but it's a beginning.

Something like 2½ billion years after the earliest life forms, evolution leads to dinosaurs, which are the dominant animal life from around t=13.450 billion to t=13.635 billion, when they suddenly disappear. (A plausible school of thought claims that modern birds are their descendants.) Mammals or their predecessors have been around since before that time, but they become more important after the extinction of the dinosaurs. The great apes appear around t=13.670 billion; the most highly developed of them are known as hominids. These are the species that most closely resemble ours. We know something about them from their fossil remains, which are still revealing species whose existence is news to us.

The Bursting Flame

For what it's worth dinosaurs were dominant for 185 million years, hominids for 30 million years, and humankind for perhaps 1½ million years so far. We have a long way to go before we can consider ourselves competitive in the longevity sweepstakes. The extinction of the dinosaurs, which made possible the emergence of mammals and eventually of humankind, required a remarkable and unpredictable cataclysmic event, as described in Appendix C.

Later, at t=13.698,360 billion, something unprecedented happens. According to Teilhard de Chardin,[88]

After thousands of years rising below the horizon, a flame bursts forth at a strictly localized point.

---

88 Teilhard de Chardin, Pierre, *The Phenomenon of Man*, translated by Bernard Wall, New York, Harper & Row, originally published in French by Editions du Seuil, Paris, 1955

Table 1: Selected Milestones in the History of Religior

Time Since t_0 (Billions of Years)	Time to Present	Event
0	13.700,000,000	Big Bang: beginning of the universe, space, and time
0.001	13.699,000,000	Beginning of galaxy formation
9.100,000,000	4.600,000,000	Planet Earth begins to coalesce
9.700,000,000	4.000,000,000	Earth cools to point where surface is solid
10.900,000,000	2.800,000,000 or earlier	First molecules capable of replicating themselves (date uncertain)
13.156,000,000	0.544,000,000	Life forms that leave fossils become abundant
13.450,000,000	0.250,000,000	Dinosaurs become the dominant creatures
13.635,000,000	0.065,000,000	Dinosaurs die out, quite abruptly; mammals begin to take over

Table 1: Selected Milestones in the History of Religion

Time Since t_0 (Billions of Years)	Time to Present	Event
13.670,000,000	0.030,000,000	Great apes appear, developing into hominids
13.698,360,000	0.001,640,000	A hominid brain leaps to consciousness: the dawning of humanity
13.699,965,000	0.000,035,000	Creation of artifacts of esthetic value: cave paintings, carvings
13.699,973,000	0.000,027,000	Possible early date for beginning of worship of The Great Goddess
13.699,991,000	0.000,009,000	Beginning of worship of The Great Goddess
13.699,997,090	0.000,002,010	Birth of Jesus of Nazareth
13.699,998,600	0.000,001,400	Beginnings of Islam
13.699,999,800	0.000,000,190	Beginnings of Church of Jesus Christ of Latter Day Saints (Mormonism)

The brain of a hominid, the most highly developed brain to that point, makes the leap to higher consciousness: in Teilhard de Chardin's term, reflection:

...the power acquired by a consciousness to turn in upon itself, to take possession of itself as an object endowed with its own particular consistence and value: no longer merely to know, but to know oneself; no longer merely to know, but to know that one knows.

In other words this hominid, which has evolved from self-replicating molecules over a period of nearly three billion years if not more, makes a crucial evolutionary step. With the rise of self-consciousness around a million and a half years ago, humanity is preparing to take its first steps into the arena it will come to dominate. Anatomical development since then has been relatively unimpressive – we don't look enormously different from the hominids of that time, though we dress better – but development of the human mind is another matter. More than a million and a half years later cave paintings and carved artifacts – not utilitarian spear points, but esthetic ornaments – begin to appear. Many of the ornaments seem to have religious connotations. In fact a sculpture of a woman with large breasts and open thighs, apparently a fertility idol, has been dated at 35,000 years ago, or t=13.699,965 billion. Civilization, culture, and religion have arrived.

So we have now skimmed the entire story from the Big Bang through appearance of some of the elements, development of galaxies and stars, creation of more elements, coalescence and solidification of Earth, isolation of continents, the appearance of life, development of mammals, consciousness. At last we have reached the beginning of humanity, which we humans see as the goal of the whole production. The stage is set for further development of culture and of religion.

The Great Goddess

Religion immediately gives rise to competing gods and in due course to the sexual proscriptions of Leviticus. Merlin Stone[89] argues

89 Stone, Merlin, *When God Was a Woman*, New York, Harcourt Brace Jovanovich, 1978

that a prominent player in the competition was The Great Goddess. There is evidence of pervasive worship of this female deity from nine thousand years ago (t=13.699,991 billion) until about the time of Jesus and beyond. An alternative view is that there were many local goddesses who eventually were subsumed into the Goddess. In either case Goddess worship has echoed through the centuries in the practice of witchcraft; it is understandable that modern Wiccans are not amused by Halloween's trivialization of witches. The Goddess has a venerable history: Stone suggests that she may even have extended back an additional eighteen thousand years, to the era of early cave paintings. Goddess worship focused on fertility: women were dominant in agriculture as well as in reproduction.

Stone tells us that in early times inheritance was matrilineal: from mother to daughter. This has important consequences, one of which is that if women are in charge attitudes to sex are likely to be quite different: monogamy becomes much less important. Monogamy (in women) is particularly important (to men) for an excellent biological reason: until recently it was the only way to be sure who is the father of a child. The message of Darwin's theory in modern language is that a child is a gene's way of making another gene. Genes that do a good job of propagating more genes like themselves continue down through the evolving generations while other genes die out. Men resulting from this evolutionary process therefore carry genes driving them to generate children and to favor their own offspring; that's how their genes are preserved. To favor his own offspring requires at a minimum that a man be able to *identify* his own offspring: those carrying his genes.

Women have the same biological imperative, of course, but the issue of identifying a woman's offspring rarely arises. (Solomon's judgment between the two women who each claimed the same baby[90] is a rare counterexample.) So women have less of a biological concern about monogamy. When inheritance came through the mother monogamy was not necessary to keep things honest. But after men

---

90 I Kings 3:16-27

challenged the matrilineal system inheritance went from father to son. Monogamy (among women) became crucial because otherwise the paternity of offspring could not be reliably known: the wrong heir might inherit. Filial identification is certain if the woman mates with only one man. Patrilineal inheritance led to a requirement that a woman be monogamous. This system was of crucial genetic importance to men, though not to women. Stone says it was facilitated by the introduction of male gods who would command the supremacy of men and the monogamy of women.

One name under which the Goddess was known was Astarte, referred to in the Bible as Ashtoreth, a male form of the name. Her brother (or possibly her son) Baal was her sexual consort. Baal also mated with a heifer, producing a divine calf. The people of Canaan before the coming of the Israelites were followers of Baal and, Stone says, of Astarte. Yahweh's followers seem to have regarded these people much as I regard the Dodgers. The Canaanite rites included sex between selected men and temple women who conceived and bore offspring. This ancient religion, with its explicit approval of sexual activity, was naturally quite attractive to some of the Israelites.

Yahweh's Competition

In the tirades against sexual license, God's people were being warned against what Yahweh's followers considered a sex cult that worshipped a female god. A man "lying with" a man as with a woman? That would make a man no more than a woman, like the woman-worshipping Canaanites! No wonder it was an abomination to the author of Leviticus. It wasn't primarily about the sex any more than my problem with my least favorite team was primarily about baseball. It was about competition and about commitment.

The Old Testament cannot be understood without recognizing the central role of the first commandment's injunction to have no other god ahead of God. Time and again the afflictions of God's people come as a punishment for idolatry. When they worship competing gods, or marry women who worship competing gods, or engage in sexual practices like those of the followers of Baal and

Astarte, they soon find themselves dispossessed and reduced to slavery. While Moses is away receiving the Ten Commandments his people worship a golden calf[91] representing the offspring of Baal's liaison with a heifer, and then engage in orgiastic revels like those of the Canaanites. Sex follows immediately after worship of the calf, and Yahweh responds with predictable rage. Syncretism, the combination of different forms of belief or practice, unleashes Yahweh's fury. He will not permit his people's exclusive devotion, and his own uniqueness, to be watered down.

Yahweh was not the first god humans worshipped, and the human understanding of God did not appear in an instant. Paul is reported to have said this to the Athenians:

The God who made the world and everything in it, he who is Lord of heaven and earth, does not live in shrines made by human hands, nor is he served by human hands, as though he needed anything, since he himself gives to all mortals life and breath and all things. From one ancestor he made all nations to inhabit the whole earth, and he allotted the times of their existence and the boundaries of the places where they would live, so that they would search for God and perhaps grope for him and find him – though indeed he is not far from each one of us.[92]

The preconscious primates could no more reflect on God than could the self-replicating molecules they evolved from. They could not grope for him, much less find him. On the timeline of the universe measured in billions of years you have to get to the fifth decimal point to see the first signs of religion. Yahweh is not known until the sixth decimal point, and when he appears he already has competitors: Yahweh was the new, improved version. Early worshippers considered him better, stronger, wiser, more effective than other gods; they didn't imagine that no other gods existed. Monotheism came later.

Karen Armstrong[93] suggests that the God of Abraham was El, a god of the Canaanites. Echoes of El appear in many Hebrew

---

91 Exodus 32:1-6

92 Acts 17:24-27

93 Armstrong, Karen, *A History of God*, New York, Ballantine Books, 1993

names, including Israel (Isra-El). There may be a long line of evolving understanding leading from the fertility Goddess as much as twenty-seven thousand years ago, through the "male" gods who took over, culminating in El who morphed into Yahweh. The morphing was probably gradual: Armstrong tells us that ancient inscriptions have been found reading, "To Yahweh and his Asherah," indicating that some people thought that Yahweh had a wife, as El did. Christians (t=13.699,998 billion) added further material to the Hebrew understanding, though of course Judaism did not disappear. Christians and Jews coexist among others with Muslims (t=13.699,998,600 billion) and Mormons (t=13.699,999,810 billion), each earlier group believing that the latest step was one step too far. All of the books of the Bible were probably written within a period of no more than thirteen hundred years ending about a century after the birth of Jesus, but there seem to be thirty-five thousand years of history, of groping, underlying that very recent spasm of writing.

Of course this does not mean that God morphed. God has revealed himself over the centuries at a pace humans could keep up with. Human understanding has progressed and, one hopes, is still progressing. We're still groping. God was originally female, if Stone is right, and later male in the biblical understanding. Today I feel confident that God has no gender but models archetypes of the best "male" and "female" characteristics. Yahweh no longer competes with Astarte, Baal, or El; each of them contributes to the current understanding of God. Faceless competitors like money and power are the current objects of idolatrous worship.

Behaving Badly

In Biblical times homosexuality was regarded as a practice, not an identity. Gene Robinson, the first openly gay Episcopal bishop, has written

It was only at the very end of the nineteenth century that the notion was first posed that there might be a certain minority of people who are naturally oriented – affectionally and sexually – toward members of the same gender.

In biblical times, and until the last hundred or so years, it's been assumed that everyone is heterosexual, which meant that anyone acting in a homosexual manner was acting "against their nature." In other words, homosexuals were "heterosexuals behaving badly." [94]

Leviticus is strongly opposed to anyone "behaving badly." The cited chapter considers it necessary to include explicit prohibitions against "uncovering the nakedness" (a euphemism for sex) of one's father, mother, father's wife, sister, father's daughter, mother's daughter, son's daughter, daughter's daughter, father's wife's daughter, father's sister, mother's sister, and so forth. Taken literally, it looks like an agenda of closing every conceivable door.

But to a large extent all this is an elaboration of the injunction against following a sex cult worshipping a false God of the wrong gender. I had the Dodgers; Yahweh's followers had the Canaanites. The command can be explicit:

Whoever lies with an animal [as Baal did] *shall be put to death.*

Whoever sacrifices to any god, other than the Lord alone, shall be devoted to destruction. [95]

These apparently disparate injunctions appear together in successive verses. In each case, the subject is not really sex, but devotion to God rather than to any competing deity.

The Old Testament seems to contain a law for every imaginable act. Some of this body of law is engagingly benevolent:

"You shall not watch your neighbor's ox or sheep straying away and ignore them; you shall take them back to their owner. If the owner does not reside near you or you do not know who the owner is, you shall bring it to your own house, and it shall remain with you until the owner claims it; then you shall return it." [96]

"You shall not withhold the wages of poor and needy laborers...you shall pay them their wages before sunset, because they are poor and their livelihood depends on them..." [97]

---

94 Robinson, Gene: *In the Eye of the Storm: Swept to the Center by God.* New York, Seabury Books, 2008

95 Exodus 22:18-19

96 Deuteronomy 22:1-3

97 Deuteronomy 24:14-15

"You shall not deprive a resident alien or an orphan of justice; you shall not take a widow's garment in pledge. Remember that you were a slave in Egypt and the Lord your God redeemed you from there; therefore I command you to do this. When you reap your harvest in the field and forget a sheaf in the field, you shall not go back and get it; it shall be left for the alien, the orphan, and the widow, so that the Lord your God may bless you in all your undertakings. When you beat your olive trees, do not strip what is left; it shall be for the alien, the orphan, and the widow." [98]

"You shall not muzzle an ox while it is treading out the grain." [99]

These are commandments to act in ways considered, then as now, models of human decency. Even animals were given the Jubilee (seventh) Year off; no one should suffer unending poverty or loss. But some of the laws are incredible to modern ears, such as those accepting slavery and misogyny, even if these laws represent a compassionate advance on what preceded them. For example:

"When you buy a male Hebrew slave, he shall serve you six years, but in the seventh he shall go out a free person, without debt. If he comes in single, he shall go out single; if he comes in married, then his wife shall go out with him. If his master gives him a wife and she bears him sons or daughters, the wife and her children shall be her master's and he shall go out alone..." [100]

Slaves got the same Jubilee as animals, but this equivalence is not a prescription that many today would accept. It has taken us a long time to hear that God was telling us not to keep slaves, that slavery really is an abomination, and that a woman is not the property of any man.

The law as given in the Pentateuch was congruent with what people of that time could understand. It has some strange passages. Enormous bloodletting of enemies is reported as a sign of Yahweh's approval of his people. We cringe today to read passages in which, at God's direction, enemies are slaughtered:

---

98 Deuteronomy 24:17-20

99 Deuteronomy 25:4

100 Exodus 21:2-4

Then they devoted to destruction by the edge of the sword all in the city, both men and women, young and old, oxen, sheep, and donkeys.[101]

Even the donkeys! What had *they* done? We think there has been progress in our understanding since this passage was written.

Moral conduct today is based on Jesus's command that we show active, creative, committed love for all of our neighbors, including our enemies. An endless series of forbidden acts in the Mosaic law was replaced by a positive message of freedom and salvation. We see that we were created to be objects of God's love and endowed with the freedom to aspire to be worthy. And that we are accepted, despite the fact that we can never on our own be acceptable, can never fulfill our aspirations. This represents a more advanced understanding of God's will than that depicted in bloodthirsty and vengeful ancient passages.

The God of Literature

Jack Miles's book, *God: A Biography*,[102] presents an interesting perspective on how God, as understood by his followers, has evolved. Miles considers God as the subject of a biography, the Bible: that is as a character in a book. Read this way God develops and changes radically, apparently as a result of his interaction with his creatures. In the opening books of the Bible he is a bloodthirsty monster. Having created humans and instructed them to "be fruitful and multiply,"[103] he decides to wipe them from the face of the earth. His reasons for doing this are vague, though it sounds as if idolatry may be at the root:

The Lord saw that the wickedness of humankind was great in the earth, and that every inclination of the thoughts of their hearts was only evil continuously[104]

He saves only Noah and Noah's household.

When he delivers his people from Egypt, God is careful to "harden his (Pharaoh's) heart"[105] so that the ruler of Egypt will

---

101 Joshua 6:21.

102 Miles, Jack: *God: A Biography*, New York, Vintage Books, 1995

103 Genesis 1:28

104 Genesis 6:5

105 Exodus 4:21 and elsewhere

not give in while successively more drastic curses are rained upon him, culminating in the slaughter of the firstborn of every family. God wants not merely to threaten this slaughter but to inflict it – to demonstrate his greatness! For the same reason he kills the entire army of Pharaoh, sparing no one. Forty years later, when it is time for his people to enter the promised land, God notes that the land is already occupied and makes it clear that mere ethnic cleansing of the present inhabitants will not satisfy him: genocide is required. And so whole cities – men, women, children, and animals – are slaughtered *at God's command*. He is enraged, and wreaks terrible vengeance upon his own people, if they show mercy to anyone. Perhaps this is because the attraction of sexual license in the religion of the Canaanites might cause intermarriage and weaken the commitment to Yahweh. And in fact that's exactly what happens.

A purely literary understanding of God makes for an absorbing book. God is, as Miles says, a character in a book. As a character he is fascinating: subject to temper tantrums, mood swings, and shifting judgments. Theists, however, don't see God as merely a literary character, but as a real and constant spirit, alive in our world though transcendent. The biblical description must then be read as our developing understanding of an unchanging God.

Unless we are to accept that God is (or was at one time) the mercurial, genocidal force described in parts of the Bible, we must see the Bible as a limited, human, and evolving record, inspired but not dictated by the Holy Spirit. In fact it must be so. Before the abyssal mystery of God as God humans can only throw up our hands. Even though he is immanent, present, available to us here, God as God is incomparably deeper than ocean depths, higher than mountain peaks, vaster than interstellar space. He is in no way to be approached *directly* by the likes of us. Our God has to be a human construct, informed by revelation but shaped by our evolving intellectual and cultural accomplishment, cumulatively expressing the most advanced understanding we can achieve at any time. With the greatest respect to the inspired authors of the Bible, I believe we are called to continue to use our minds and hearts creatively to gain better understanding of what is expected of us.

Christ's New Standard

In this spirit we can see that the Old Testament injunctions regarding sex have more to do with forbidding worship of sexually permissive gods like Baal and Astarte/Ashtoreth – or any other gods – than with forbidding sexual practices. Prohibiting certain forms of physical friction while commanding others ("be fruitful and multiply") makes no sense. To see an injunction against idolatry three millennia ago as a commandment about sex today is to miss the point. Idolatry is the focus, not sex in itself. Of course today Baal is out of style, but it is still true that some of our idolatry is focused on sex. This idolatry, like all idolatry, is forbidden to us: we are to love God with our *whole* hearts. But it's the idolatry that is the problem, not the sex.

In the New Testament, Jesus sets out a new standard. He collapses all of the detailed instructions of the Pentateuch into an understanding that we are to act with our neighbor's best interests as our focus. Not that idolatry has disappeared. Nobody talks about Baal any more but it's easy – too easy – to name some of the idols that surround us: wealth, power, fame, and as noted that favorite of Baal's (and Yahweh's) followers, sex. These *acts* are not forbidden: we can earn money, run for office, accomplish deeds that make us well known, even make love if we do it lovingly. But the *worship* of these acts is forbidden to us, as worship of Baal is forbidden in Leviticus, because we are commanded to love God with our whole hearts and our neighbor as ourselves. Leviticus has the big idea right; it is only the details that don't speak to the modern condition.

This commandment to love is not conditional and will not become obsolete. Most of us would understand today, as an obvious corollary, that slavery and genocide are radically excluded. When Exodus was written this was not the general human understanding. But God's understanding does not change. If we are correct in thinking that slavery and genocide are radically excluded today,

God knew them to be radically excluded then. The compassionate limitations on slavery described in Exodus were a human advance but fell far short of what we today understand to be God's will. At least in some respects our understanding today has come to resemble God's more closely than did that of the authors of Exodus. These examples show that the past three thousand years have not been entirely devoid of progress: moral understanding can surpass that of the authors of passages in the Bible. We are not to *worship* sex or any other idol; we may *practice* them when they are consistent with the law of love. And of course today's understanding will develop further. Humans do not have the final answers, and will not in this sphere of being. But the commandment to love is not a human artifice. It is from Christ and it is good for all time.

There are people who feel that this new standard of Christ's sets the bar too low. Their objections are not a new development. Over the centuries, churches have constantly invented rules of behavior and have generally defined acts breaking these rules as sins. There are endless examples of things congregants have been forbidden to do at one time or another. These rules almost always contained some grain of sense in them, though nothing to justify making them into categorical prohibitions. Here is a small random sample:

Dancing: might lead to lustful thoughts followed by God knows what

Dancing particular dances (at one time the waltz, later whatever new movement seemed most provocative): same reason

Playing cards: encourages gambling, which focuses on mammon, encourages slothful shortcuts rather than honest toil

Drinking alcohol: drunkenness followed by untold evils

Certain soft drinks, coffee, and tea: unhealthy

Playing or listening to rock and roll music – later rap music (and earlier, jazz): see dancing

Provocative clothing (especially if worn by women): see dancing

Going to the movies: exposes one to ungodly ideas

And so forth. All of the objections raised are valid to one degree or another. Any of these actions might be a bad idea in certain circumstances; in fact every one of them can be highly toxic. But that is a matter for human judgment. Most adults can drink alcohol in moderation with enjoyment and without dire consequences. Children and alcoholics cannot. A person about to drive a car is irresponsible if he consumes much alcohol, and by placing lives at risk he clearly violates the law of love. An alcoholic who drinks is likely to forfeit much of what gives his life meaning, with grave consequences for those close to him. A parent who fails to protect his children from experiences for which they are not ready has no place in a civilized society. We don't need a law – *it's a sin to take a drink* – to cover this behavior. The commandment to love is enough. An adult who considers the consequences of his actions in the light of this commandment may choose to drink, but will not commit the damaging acts sometimes associated with drinking.

The Moral Absolute

A serious, creative, thoughtful application of the commandment is enough for other situations where people like to define sins. For example, most Christians accept that love comes from God. Now when two people, of the same or opposite sexes, are joined in a devoted and committed relationship of significant duration, that relationship must be assumed to be informed by love. They are not "behaving badly"; they are expressing their identity, and their love. But if love comes from God, a relationship informed by love must have been blessed by God:

> ...*God is love, and those who abide in love abide in God, and God abides in them.*[106]

And if blessed by God, the relationship should have no trouble gaining acceptance from mere humans. It should be a rare bishop, priest, or parishioner who would dare to condemn a relationship blessed by God. Yet these birds do exist – and are not rare. They choose the verse quoted above from Leviticus, a short passage from Deuteronomy, another from Romans, and a few other fragments, and construct a commandment. They ignore the fact that most of these

---

106 1 John 4:16

citations are couched in the context of an insistence that God's people must worship no other God: that homosexuality was often a part of the worship practice of pagan deities. It is in the course of destroying pagan idols that many of the slaughters of the Old Testament occur.

When Jesus said, "I am come...to fulfill (the law),"[107] he was not talking about the imperfect efforts of humans, however inspired, to understand God's law. Jesus demonstrates God's law as it is meant to be understood. He does so in the most direct way imaginable: by living and teaching the law of love, by displaying in his very being that he is the incarnation of meaning and that the meaning is love. This does not contradict God's law in the Old Testament but it shines the light of meaning on all efforts to understand.

Not all relationships between people of the same sex are informed by love. They can be brief, coercive, exploitative, brutally one-sided: loveless. Such relationships are not blessed by God and they are likely to be damaging to the participants. But this is not a condemnation of same-sex relationships; it is a condemnation of loveless relationships, which are tragically common among heterosexuals as well. Leviticus does not make this distinction because Leviticus is really thinking about Baal, not Cupid. Jesus makes the distinction: his focus is love. To abandon the positive message of Jesus for the older message of injunctions and threats is a perversion of the essence of Christianity. Baal is no longer a major problem, though idolatry certainly is.

More generally, it is a mistake to cling to the old understanding of morality as a series of rules that must not be broken. The commandment to love is the moral absolute, but its application can change over the course of time. Some acts that violated Christ's commandment in the past no longer have that effect because conditions have changed. At one time, for example, to have carnal knowledge of a woman before marriage was to subject her to heavy societal penalties. If you look long enough ago, or far enough away in current times, she could even face death by stoning. (The penalty, if any, for her partner was and is usually lighter.) Even where stoning

---

107 Matthew 5:17

is no longer a threat, she might be excluded from the approval of her community and participation in its activities, disowned by her family, and forced to move to a new area where her disgrace was not known. Further, either or both parties might experience the act of sex as sinful because of the societal strictures, and suffer psychological harm. And certainly there is loveless sex, as described above, that is against the participants' interests.

Under any of those circumstances sex might well be inconsistent with the commandment to love, because it resulted in great pain for one or both participants. Today, there are many places and situations where these objections no longer describe current conditions. There are still serious issues, of psychology, immaturity, unstable commitment, deception, betrayal, and many others. But these are all conditional objections, matters for thoughtful consideration by mature individuals. (Sex should not be for children, though attempts to stop them have not been conspicuously successful.) The act of sex does not *in itself* estrange one from God or from one's fellows. Nor does the absence of sex legitimize a relationship characterized by the tragic distortions described above.

Again, it was until quite recently scandalous for unmarried persons to live together. Today this behavior is common and is accepted in many families, even when it is assumed that sex is occurring. Many conditional concerns arise. The halfway position of living together but not committing to a permanent relationship can lead to great pain, particularly if the two parties do not have the same strength of feeling about each other or the same expectations. If the woman gets pregnant the child may not be properly cared for. Economic issues can arise. But while there are many reasons to think carefully and creatively before entering into such a relationship, it is not a fundamental diminution of moral standards for this behavior to occur. It is simply a response to changing conditions. It may or may not be – often, no doubt, it is – an unfortunate choice for many couples, but that is a matter of individual judgment. After all quite a few of the same concerns arise within marriage. Living together is not inherently an expression of sin any more than marriage is.

We have not been engaging in a description of moral relativism. The moral imperative is absolute and unchanging: love God and your neighbor, God's child, so that you express this love by acting in your neighbor's best interest. If conditions change, making an act that was damaging in other circumstances into one that is harmless, the moral weight can indeed change. Pork was forbidden to ancient Jews under the same code of ritual purity that condemned homosexual relations. Improperly prepared pork could be unhealthy. Christians and many modern Jews believe that eating pork is acceptable because we now know how to prepare this meat so that it is healthful. The moral weight of an action can be relative because of changes in societal conditions, even though the one moral rule is eternal and absolute. Scripture needs to be read in the light of this understanding.

CHAPTER 12:
Freedom and Salvation

The message of Jesus, then, is not a series of injunctions against doing things. The law of the Old Testament is largely couched in negative terms – "Thou shalt not…" – but Jesus brought a different understanding. His teaching is both easier and harder: easier to remember and harder to follow. Instead of a law that prescribed in detail what we must avoid, he reduced everything to a pair of simple commands: "Love the Lord" and "Love your neighbor." No laws to memorize and obey, no long books filled with anathema. Christians don't have to look it up. We know what we are commanded to do and the command is positive: "Do this" rather than "Don't do that."

The trouble is we *can't* do it. The message of Jesus is simple but it's not easy. Most of us rarely have a problem with "You shall not murder." That's easy – usually. But not one of us loves his neighbor as himself, loves as Jesus loved. The Old Testament understanding was cut and dried, highly prescriptive, suitable for children. The medieval church took a similar attitude, with detailed prescriptions about all aspects of conduct. But Jesus didn't come to prepare humankind for the Middle Ages. He came to free us from a preoccupation with detailed requirements and to substitute something simpler, more profound, and much more difficult: get out there and *do* something. His approach requires a creative adult participation that goes far beyond refraining from murder. We are expected to care for our neighbor – clearly defined by the parable of the Good Samaritan to include everyone on the planet – on the basis of an intense love. We are to feed him when he is hungry, clothe him when he is naked, visit him when he is alone, tell him God loves him when he is in prison. We are constantly to seek ways to help him grow into his destiny, to reach his full potential. If we could manage all that, it would scarcely be necessary to add the final reminder: "Oh by the way, don't murder him."

Not only do we find it impossible to love our neighbor in the way that Jesus intended: we can't even love ourselves in that way. The task of Jesus was to reconcile us to God, to our neighbor, and to ourselves: I am my own closest neighbor. For this purpose we need to remember how important we are. God created us because he needed objects for his love. If he could love us it should be possible for us to live with ourselves, respect ourselves, value ourselves. Our chemistry is mundane but our souls are unique: like snowflakes but infinitely more valuable. The bumper sticker that says "Smile: Jesus loves you" makes the key point.

Mankind's Response

Our love of God and our fellows is incomplete. But we don't have to wait for perfection – it would be a long wait. When Professor Tillich told me God created us because he is a creative principle, I asked what our response should be. I can't quote him half a century later, but in effect he said we should seek closer relationships with each other. This understanding of "Love your neighbor" makes love into an active verb, not a mere passive emotion: something we do rather than just something we feel. If we can't love as Jesus loved, we can express love by visiting the sick, feeding the hungry, expressing in our actions the perfect love to which we aspire. The message of Jesus is that God loves us and wants us to love God and each other. Everything he tells us is positive. To paraphrase: "Keep your priorities straight, protect the weak, support people rather than condemning them. Follow me. Rejoice! The news is good. The bread of life is among you and never dies."

Jesus was asked what must be done to inherit eternal life. The questioner insisted that he had kept the commandments since his youth. Jesus crushed him by replying, "You lack one thing; go, sell what you own, and give the money to the poor..."[108] Jesus wasn't

---

108 Mark 10:21

talking about embracing poverty for its own sake. He was talking about commitment. He was saying, "Sell out what is ephemeral and devote yourself to what is essential." Jesus was not a moral relativist; his morality was absolute. But it was brief. *All* that we are commanded to do is to love, actively, creatively, as Jesus loved. The rest follows.

Larry Kramer, a playwright and gay activist, caught the flavor in a speech reported in *The New Yorker*:

It takes hard work to behave like an adult. It takes discipline. You want it to be simple. It isn't simple. Yes, it is. Grow up. Behave responsibly. Fight for your rights. Take care of yourself and each other. These are the answers. It takes courage to live.[109]

So it is gross perversion to turn the message of Jesus into a threat of doom. John the Baptist raged at his listeners, condemning them as a brood of vipers and calling on them to get ready to follow a new path – to repent – and to look for the One who was coming. But the approach of Jesus was different. He did not routinely call his followers by unpleasant names. It is true that he was stern with the Scribes and Pharisees because they were the ones to whom much had been given and from whom much was demanded. Besides, he was speaking of elements of their practice that were hypocritical and corrupt, and Jesus was the purifier. He was violent, though not damagingly so, in cleansing the temple of exploiters, and again the thrust was positive: God's house must be respected. But he was not fierce to the little sinners, the adulterers and corrupt tax collectors and prostitutes. He loved them, although their actions did not meet with his approval. He was willing to dine with them in the face of rabid criticism. The experience of Jesus brought them healing in mind and body. We may presume that they went on to live better lives than would have resulted from a fire and brimstone denunciation. The story of the wedding at Cana suggests that Jesus was a good man to have at a party.

---

109 Michael Specter "Nowhere" (The Talk of the Town) *The New Yorker*, November 22, 2004

Jesus, the Christ, is the incarnation of the meaning of being and everything about him is positive. Even sweating blood in the garden of Gethsemane, he accepted that the events of Calvary must be embraced on the way to Easter. The religion based on the Christ cannot be couched in negative terms. Jesus didn't say, "Don't kill, don't steal, don't have sex." If you hear him in those terms you are deaf to his positive message, which was to *love* your neighbor, *help* the poor, *act* to strengthen your lover's heart rather than break it. It wasn't "Don't make money." It was to concentrate your heart on what is most important. In other words have no other gods. Jesus validated the Old Testament injunction against idolatry but dropped the detailed codes to focus on the essentials. And the thrust, as he told us to make good decisions, was never "Don't enjoy life," What he said was, "...I came that they may have life, and have it abundantly."[110]

Culture Games

This may sound simple but it's a difficult message and a creative response to it takes work. Jesus is the Word, the final revelation, but though the revelation is final our understanding of it is not. We have seen that revelation at a given time cannot go beyond what humankind is able to receive. The Bible contains centuries of progressive revelation showing the development of Jewish thought. Yahweh starts as one of many tribal gods, in competition with the others and willing to kill followers of his rivals. Abraham announces that there is only one god, a bedrock principle today for Jews, Christians, and Muslims. The facts about God didn't change – there was always only one God – but mankind's understanding evolved.

Robert Wright[111] has discussed this developing understanding as a function of cultural evolution. Moving forward from Darwin's description of biological evolution as the development of species in response to challenges to the organism, we now understand that the unit of biological evolution is the gene. Analogously, the *meme* has

---

110 John 10:10
111 Wright, Robert, *The Evolution of God*, New York, Little, Brown and Company, 2009

been defined as the unit of cultural evolution. If a meme responds constructively to challenges facing a society it will help that society to thrive. Such memes are more likely to be propagated over time, like genes that lead to individual survival.

We think we know quite a bit about the earliest societies. The knowledge is based on study of primitive societies that persist into historical time, and on archeological findings, the analogy to fossils. In the picture Wright sketches, biological evolution comes first: it has been going on for billions of years and obviously modern large organisms don't look like the single-celled bacteria of the earliest stages. Societies also change, of course. Hunter-gatherer societies were simple and small, largely conditioned by biological evolution. People who were quick to avenge injuries and suspicious of intruders from outside the clan had a survival advantage. Hostility was a useful meme at first. But as the small villages of just a few dozen people merged into larger chiefdoms, the role of cultural memes increased. Harmonious relations with other clans within the chiefdom led to a stronger society, and xenophobia was less favored. Nation states, the next step up in size and complexity, had still more reason to seek peace within the state and with other states, particularly with potential trading partners.

This effect is formalized in game theory. A game is a transaction between two individuals or groups and is characterized by a score for each participant. Positive scores represent a favorable result, negative scores an unfavorable result. The sum is the total of the scores for the two participants. A zero-sum game is one in which A can increase his score only by causing B's score to decrease. For example, if A steals B's spear, A's score at that point is positive to the extent that B's score is negative and the sum is zero. Negative sums are also possible: if as the game proceeds B resents the theft of his spear and both die in the resulting fight, both scores are negative and the sum is negative. But trade, for example, can benefit both sides and give a positive sum. When states see their relationships as nonzero-sum – as positive – they understand the value of getting along. As such states do indeed prosper, cultural evolution will favor harmonious memes.

Harmonious memes affect the emergence of more sophisticated religions. As Wright sees it, the early hunter-gatherer societies had many gods to account for the many environmental challenges, but a god's influence was local. Then over time the effects of trade and of war caused the group's wellbeing to depend on broader positive-sum relationships, first outside the family, later outside the tribe, still later outside the nation. War is clearly worse than zero sum: the winner, if there is a winner, almost always gains less than the loser loses. Positive sum situations are those, like trade, in which both sides benefit. According to Wright, recognition of the mutual advantage of these relationships led states to grease the wheels by showing respect for each other's gods. In time foreign gods could be accepted into a state's pantheon and their gods considered to extend their protection more widely.

Wright believes that the Israelites were initially polytheistic, respecting their own gods and the gods of nations with which they had useful relations. A further step was to merge foreign and domestic gods. Gods became more versatile and fewer in number as people concentrated on the most successful deities. But when the international scene grew hostile, as happened regularly then as now, the other nation's gods might be rejected and eventually deemed nonexistent. Gods of conquered nations might be absorbed into the dominant nation's chief god, pacifying the vanquished by letting them continue something akin to their traditional worship. The endpoint of the process was monotheism. In this view monotheism was not a divine revelation to Abraham but a developing response to "facts on the ground," Wright's term for tangible internal and external factors. Wright even argues that God's injunction to love all people did not come from Jesus as experienced by his contemporaries, but was a response to facts on the ground, and was first enunciated by St. Paul decades after Jesus's death. Religious progress, which we have seen as evolving from our groping and the Holy Spirit's revelation, is in this view a function of the evolution of cultures as they became increasingly affected by worldwide events, rather than only by local ones.

Some of Wright's assertions may be shocking to those of us brought up in the conventional church view, and he may or may not be correct about the events he discusses. The history surrounding things that happened two or three millennia ago is murky, and it is possible to doubt that the historical approach will ever give definitive answers. (After studying the question, Tillich concluded that it never would.) Yet Wright's approach can be seen as a different perspective on the evolving understanding we have been discussing. He sees a progression toward a positive sum moral order that he considers the only hope for saving present civilization from annihilating itself. He believes this to be possibly an order that has been evolving under divine inspiration, though he doesn't mention the Holy Spirit by name. To this extent his approach parallels the progressive groping we have been discussing. On the basis of cultural evolution, Wright suggests a history of this groping by "people of the book": Hebrews, early Christians, and Muslims.

Ongoing Revelation

Regardless of the extent to which Wright's picture is correct, the Bible must be read as an ongoing, evolving revelation. In its totality it contains the word of God. Yet it is a record of the progressing human understanding over a period of time, rather than a transcription of God's infallible dictation. It's a slideshow, not a snapshot. There's no sense in reading a single short passage, much less a single verse, and trying to extract from it a divine command that must be followed without question in a radically changed environment. In fact no one does this consistently with biblical passages. We all cherry-pick passages to fit our views. It is tragically common to hear a short citation presented as a categorical answer and particularly as a "thou shalt not." Jesus didn't function that way, except when he was sparring with opponents and showing that he could play the game better than they.[112]

---

112 Matthew 22:23-33

In the Gospel of Matthew,[113] Jesus paints a positive eschatological picture for his disciples, in which the king, Jesus, commends those who have followed him and places them at his right hand.

Then the king will say to those at his right hand, "Come, you that are blessed by my Father, inherit the kingdom prepared for you from the foundation of the world; for I was hungry and you gave me food, I was thirsty and you gave me something to drink, I was a stranger and you welcomed me, I was naked and you gave me clothing, I was sick and you took care of me, I was in prison and you visited me."

Then the righteous will answer him, "Lord, when was it that we saw you hungry and gave you food, or thirsty and gave you something to drink? And when was it that we saw you a stranger and welcomed you, or naked and gave you clothing? And when was it that we saw you sick or in prison and visited you?"

And the king will answer them, "Truly I tell you, just as you did it to one of the least of these who are members of my family, you did it to me."

This judgment is not reserved for end times. We are called to these actions based on the commandment to love, right now. As followers of Jesus we don't determine morality by asking, "Did a tribesman in an ancient culture understand God to condemn this act?" Rather, we ask, "What will this do for my neighbor/husband/wife/child/lover? Will it help that person, and me, and our community, in today's world, to develop as loving, supporting, creative participants in the New Being?" When we know that, the moral question is answered.

God and Santa Claus

The task of the Holy Spirit is to help us to understand, and it's a huge task. There is so much that seems incomprehensible. Interviewed at a time when he considered his death imminent, South African Archbishop Desmond Tutu was asked what question he would put to God. He replied, "Why, God, did you make suffering so central to everything? Why? Why? Why?"

"And what will his answer be?"

"God says, 'I obviously had the choice of making all kinds of different worlds, but I wanted to make a world of creatures who

---

113 Matthew 25:34-41

would love me, who would choose to love me, and that would not have been the case if they had been automatons. They had to have free will: they had to be free. And this is how they have used their freedom . . .' "

As Archbishop Tutu understood, God is not Santa Claus. Tutu was not the first to ask, "How could a loving God allow horrible things?" God accepts us, but we have to accept that he is not always comprehensible to us. God does not cradle us against all disasters; he opts for freedom. One fact we know about God is that he tolerates crib death. Perhaps he sometimes prevents this disaster – maybe the Holy Spirit warns parents – but he doesn't always prevent it. It happens in his universe, to some parents but not others. Parents who pray for their children to be spared from this fate must express their prayer concretely by learning everything possible about how to avoid it. Crib death cannot be understood in terms of the gentle paternalism taught in Sunday school. We live in a universe where unspeakable things happen. God does not prevent them; he is not that kind of God. He does not do things the way we imagine we would do them if we were God.

This is not to suggest that God deliberately afflicts us with agonizing tests. He does not send plagues, or war, or drought to see whether our coping skills have progressed to the point where we can deal with disaster. Most of the time we are responsible for our own afflictions. Sometimes they just happen: stuff happens. But remember, we need to be free and independent *others* if we are to be the objects of God's love. The Creator wants more from us than the sheltered existence of sheep. We are accountable for the kinds of lives we live.

In this we are different from other animals. If a tiger kills half the residents of a village he does not transgress any moral code. He is carnivorous, he has long claws, he is hungry. What he does is what he must do; like Martin Luther before the Diet of Worms, he can do no other. The surviving villagers may have to band together to kill the tiger in the interest of public safety, but they should do this with regret and without rancor. They have no right to blame him. He has no moral responsibility. It seems bizarre to use the term "sock puppet" to refer to so magnificent a creature as a tiger, but in large measure his actions are automatic, not independent, not truly free.

We of the human species do not escape responsibility for our actions. We do have free will, and if our freedom is far from perfect, it is by no means purely illusory. Freedom requires the potential for unspeakable things to happen, and this potential is real only if unspeakable things sometimes do happen. It seems that to allow us to be more free than tigers God must tolerate crib death.

Humans often fail to use our freedom constructively, as Archbishop Tutu also understood. A typical institutional response has been to try to eliminate the opportunity to fail. That's why religious and governmental institutions set up indices of forbidden experiences, books, films, thoughts. They assume that one will be a better (or more tractable) human if one never falls, even if the reason is that one is never tempted. That is not God's approach. A tiger is never tempted: he does what he does without introspection. This is his limitation. A human achieves something only he when exercises his freedom to rise above opportunities to do wrong and courageously does what is right. If his input is censored – even leaving aside the question of what earthly power has the right to decide what is best for him to hear and see – his opportunity to succeed is diminished. One does not grow by staying out of pitfalls one has no opportunity to fall into. The important thing is the growth, not the staying out of pitfalls.

Other animals are to a great degree creatures of their destiny. They do not ponder deep meanings; they are not aware of the Holy Spirit. Since their will rarely goes beyond fundamental needs of survival and reproduction, what freedom they have is very limited. But when God created humans as objects for his love he did not create sock puppets. Because we have a deeper consciousness we are more free: we are *other* than God and so are fit objects of God's love. That means we are responsible.

It is a distortion to say, when death, disease, and calamity strike, that it is God's will. God does not micromanage our lives in this way. It is, for example, a particular blasphemy to state that the AIDS epidemic is God's judgment on homosexuals. God does not create us to torture us. It is God's will that we have a considerable degree of freedom, with the inescapable consequence that we can do terrible things to ourselves and each other. It is God's will that we are mortal, allowing for growth and renewal and for individual graduation to a new plane of being. It is not specifically God's will that a disease, or a war, or a tsunami slaughter hundreds of thousands of human beings. It is God's will that we live in a universe where such things *can* happen, and, according to Murphy's Law,[114] they *do* happen.

The Gods' Ring and Human Freedom

A parallel perspective on the value and the costs of human freedom can be seen in Richard Wagner's operatic cycle, *The Ring of the Niebelung*. Wagner depicts Wotan, the father of the gods, seeking to create independent humans. His reason is different from God's reason for creating independent *others*; Wotan needs someone other than a god to return the ring to the Rhine maidens and…oh never mind why. The point is that one after another his attempts fail. His creations are pale reflections of himself, not free and independent entities, not *others*. "Varlets are all I can make," he complains despairingly in one translation. But finally his machinations bear fruit. Shocking incestuous shenanigans among his descendants lead to the birth of Siegfried, his grandson. (Wotan is *both* of Siegfried's grandfathers, maternal and paternal: Siegfried's parents are Wotan's twin son and daughter, Siegmund and Sieglinde, who in turn are the issue of Wotan's adulterous liaison with a human woman. Brünnhilde – the one with the horned helmet in the operas – is the half-sister of Siegmund and Sieglinde and is Siegfried's lover as well as his aunt. No one can deny that Wagner thought outside the box.)

To make it possible for Siegfried to grow up free, Wotan avoids all contact with the boy, whose mother died in childbirth and whose

---

114 Murphy's Law is a classic principle; I don't know where it comes from. It states, "If a thing can go wrong, it will." Its application can help one to anticipate and avoid great evils. Imagine the disaster that could have been avoided if oil well drilling had always been conducted with due regard for Murphy's Law.

father died the day after Siegfried's conception. Brought up by the dwarf Mime, Siegfried reaches adulthood unaware of his relationship with Wotan, and learns to fend for himself. When they eventually meet Siegfried expresses his autonomy by defying Wotan, breaking the god's mighty spear and establishing his own independence. Wotan has managed to create a free human, but only at the cost of ending his own absolute power. The era of the gods' supremacy will give way to the era of humans.

God doesn't lose any of his power when he gives us the freedom to make independent decisions, but in making us free *others* he renounces the strategy of preventing us from making tragic mistakes. We have seen that the processes of life, complex as they are, are normal chemistry. Like other chemical processes, they depend primarily on forces acting between tiny particles carrying an electric charge. Cut and dried as it may sound, this does not stand in the way of our freedom, our otherness. Chemistry and physics do not make us into automatons whose actions are predestined. Even in their own domain, they do not determine precisely what will happen. Physical insights of the last century make this clear.

The Predictable Universe

Through the Nineteenth Century, Isaac Newton's synthesis of the laws of mechanics and James Clerk Maxwell's synthesis of the laws of electromagnetism seemed, in a certain sense, to have taken freedom out of the universe. On the largest scale, the motions of celestial bodies could be predicted very accurately: knowing where each planet is at a single instant, for example, it became possible to predict where they would all be at any future time. The calculation is far from simple but it can be done. On a smaller scale, the motions of, say, billiard balls could be calculated in similar detail. This had a troubling consequence. Suppose one knew the precise state of the universe at one instant, including the position and velocity of every last particle and the details of every electrical charge and electromagnetic field. That's a lot to know, but the information apparently existed – every particle had a well-defined position and velocity – even if no one knew all the answers. And if one did know all that, then every physical event to follow through to the end of time could be predicted: the entire future of the universe would be laid bare. The computation would be too large ever to be performed in real life but the answer would exist. Even though we couldn't really perform the calculation, it's clear that the calculation *has* a solution and that every detail of the future is calculable. This has a deep philosophical consequence: we no longer have any freedom. We might have the illusion of free will, but in reality the future is fixed and unchangeable by anything we can do. The universe is a complicated but totally predictable clockwork mechanism. That's the depressing prediction of classical physics.

Then, beginning late in the Nineteenth Century, physics experienced a revolution beginning with recognition of a problem that had no obvious connection to issues of free will. It was known that every object radiates electromagnetic energy at a variety of wavelengths. Hotter objects produce more radiation and at shorter wavelengths, but every object emits radiation. Physicists needed to be able to calculate this phenomenon because that's what physicists do. But they soon noticed that the classical theoretical treatment could not possibly be right. Accepted theory led to the absurd prediction that each object would emit an *infinite* amount of short wavelength radiation. This situation is known as the ultraviolet catastrophe, because short wavelength light is in the ultraviolet band. Obviously the theory needed to be corrected: nothing can emit an infinite amount of energy. The calculation had been done correctly in terms of what was known; it wasn't a matter of someone making a mistake. Instead, the discrepancy showed that theorists must be making some hidden assumption that led to the incorrect result. The question was, what mistaken assumption was being made?

In 1900 the German physicist Max Planck (1858-1947) published the answer. It had been assumed that energy could be radiated continuously, in amounts as large or small as were needed. Planck showed that theory matches experiment if one drops the assumption of continuous radiation. Instead, energy must be emitted in discrete packets. Each packet, called a quantum, contains a precisely defined energy that depends only on the wavelength. For any wavelength, one quantum represents the smallest amount of energy that can be emitted. Larger amounts of energy are radiated by emitting a larger number of quanta. The energy of one quantum is very small, so in ordinary situations we detect a huge number of them and don't notice that the radiation is not continuous. They're like tiny grains of sand. But physicists had to give up the picture of energy being emitted like a continuous stream of liquid, and accept that it came off in grains. Planck's theory announced the revolution and signaled the end of the classical physics of the Nineteenth Century.

Planck's quantum concept had wider applications. Neils Bohr (1885-1962) applied it to the physics of atoms, where another unresolved problem existed. On a classical picture an atom's electrons were thought to revolve around the nucleus, held by the attraction of the positively charged nucleus but prevented from falling into the nucleus by centrifugal force. It's analogous to planets revolving around the sun, but there's an important difference: electrons carry an electric charge. An electron traveling in a circle is effectively a radio antenna, radiating energy continuously. The electron would therefore gradually lose energy, travel more slowly, experience less centrifugal force, and be pulled into the nucleus. This process would play out in less than a second. All atoms would be unstable and would by now have disappeared. This is obviously not what we observe.

The problem was analogous to the ultraviolet catastrophe: it was another case where doing the physics right (according to classical principles) led to a result that was clearly wrong. And it had a related solution. Bohr resolved the problem of stable atoms through the use of the quantum concept. He postulated that an atomic electron can travel only in certain allowed orbits, each of which has a defined energy. The electron can move from a lower to a higher energy orbit by absorbing a quantum of light whose energy makes up the energy difference between the two orbits. Alternatively, it can emit a quantum of radiation of the same energy, and move from a higher to a lower energy orbit. But it can't lose energy in smaller amounts than this quantum energy: it can't lose energy gradually and spiral into the nucleus. By imposing a minimum in radiated energy Bohr was able to model a stable atom.

The End of Predictability

Now we're coming to the question of free will. Quantum theory became central to several emerging areas of physics in addition to those addressed by Planck and Bohr. Many physicists including Werner Heisenberg (1901-1976) worked on elaborating the quantum theory itself, building the theoretical edifice of quantum mechanics that dominates modern physics and successfully describes the behavior of very small objects. A defining moment came in 1927, when Heisenberg stated an important fundamental principle at the core of quantum mechanics and named it in his native German *unbestimmtheit*. This is often translated "uncertainty" but a better rendering is "indeterminacy."[115] Heisenberg effectively announced that freedom had been introduced into the physical world.

The principle of indeterminacy is a statement about limitations on measurements. We can measure the position of an electron, for example, as accurately as our instruments and ingenuity permit. There's no fundamental limit. We can also measure the electron's velocity with unlimited accuracy. Heisenberg's principle kicks in when we want to know *both* of these values at the same time. Now there is a limit: the more accurately we measure the position, the less we know about the velocity. If we measure the position exactly we give up all knowledge about the velocity. This has nothing to do with how accurately our instruments work; rather it states that exact values of position and velocity cannot *exist* simultaneously. Bizarre as it seems, this principle has been supported by every relevant experiment

---

115 The German word *bestimmt* means "fixed"; *bestimmtheit* means "fixedness" and *unbestimmtheit* means the opposite. The form "unfixedness" is unknown in English, but "indeterminacy" supplies a good translation. The alternative, "uncertainty," suggests incorrectly that there is a fixed value but we don't know it.

and must be accepted to the extent that any scientific statement is accepted: that is, until contradicted by new evidence.

The practical reason for the limitation is that in order to make these measurements we must interact with the particle. The act of measuring changes the thing being measured. Suppose we measure the position exactly, which we might accomplish by hitting the electron with a beam of light. But the light causes the particle to rebound, changing its velocity so we don't know how fast it's moving. To make the position measurement as accurate as possible we use light of short wavelength. But the shorter the wavelength the higher the energy of one quantum of light, called a photon, and the more we change the velocity of the particle. If the particle's velocity cannot in any way be precisely known after the position measurement, then at that point it does not *have* a defined velocity. The more precisely the position is measured the less precisely the velocity can be known, and vice versa.

Quantum theory shows that the effect does not depend on how the measurement is made; it is universally true that position and velocity are not both fixed at any given time. It's important to understand that the exact velocity is not merely unknown to us; rather, if the particle's position is fixed its velocity is undetermined even in principle. The particle doesn't know; God himself doesn't know. Since the particle's velocity is not determined there is no way of predicting where it will be a second from now. It does not possess a fixed future. If it is going a hundred miles a second – not especially fast for an electron – and nothing interferes, it will be a hundred miles away after a second. If it is going one millimeter a second it will be only a millimeter away. In a certain sense quantum mechanics says that the electron possesses both of these futures, and everything in between, simultaneously.

We have seen that electrons are central to chemical reactions. If it is impossible even for God to predict where a single electron will be one second from now, obviously he cannot tell which chemical reactions out of all those possible will occur at each point in space after fourteen billion years. God is not ignorant; the future simply is not fixed. We saw in Chapter 7 the reason, from a theist's perspective, why we must have free will. Now we see, contrary to what was believed for a long time, that this freedom has a counterpart in modern physics. This is not a limitation of God's omniscience; it is the way he designed the universe. God knew all about the Heisenberg principle long before Heisenberg discovered it. A theist might describe indeterminacy as God's way of granting us freedom.

Indeterminacy and Chaos

The effects of indeterminacy are substantial only for very small objects such as electrons. Something as large as a billiard ball, or even a grain of sand, is not affected significantly, so we can measure position and velocity well enough to play billiards or make sand castles. You don't have to try to drive a car under conditions where you can't tell where other objects are because they look fuzzy, and you don't know how fast you are moving. Indeterminacy plays no apparent role in activities of daily life, but for small enough objects the effect is dominant.

Despite its limitation to the tiny, the effects of indeterminacy can produce major echoes in the world we experience. An example concerns radioactivity, such as emission of an α (pronounced "alpha") particle from inside an atomic nucleus. The α particle, a grouping of two protons and two neutrons all stuck tightly together by the strong nuclear force, is the nucleus of a helium atom. (It has no electrons orbiting outside it, so it doesn't act like helium chemically.) This entity can be contained within a larger atomic nucleus and can later be expelled from that nucleus. This emission is completely controlled by the principle of indeterminacy: the α is strongly attached to the interior of the nucleus and, without indeterminacy, could never get out at all. One can measure the average time between α's coming out of a sample of radioactive nuclei, but cannot tell when a particular nucleus will emit an α. If a scientist had a particle counter next to a source of α he could easily count the number of α detected in a given time and so measure the strength of the source. But even God could not say, "The next α is coming out of *this* nucleus…right *now*." It's not that he doesn't know. The problem is that the time for the next α to come is indeterminate:

the information doesn't exist. There is no way to predict just when the number on the particle counter's display would change.

We can concoct a hypothetical example of real consequences of Heisenberg's principle as applied to α particle emission. Suppose two bored graduate students are studying α emission from a radioactive source so weak that there's only one count per minute. That's an average: sometimes the interval may be less than half a minute, other times more than two minutes. The students have a very common experimental setup comprising a detector system surrounding the source and a display showing the total number of α particles detected so far. In a late night session – that's what graduate students are for – they place a bet on whether the counts will reach a total of one thousand before or after midnight. If it happens before midnight Joe can take the rest of the night off; otherwise Jim gets to go home. As it happens the counts reach one thousand at ten seconds before midnight. Joe wins the bet, sets off for home, and is hit by a truck. At one minute before twelve there would have been no way to predict which student would have his career truncated by this tragedy. This does not mean that God can play no role. The Holy Spirit could whisper in Joe's ear a suggestion that he stay in the lab and keep his colleague company, but Joe's decision would be his own.

If this example seems artificial, remember that what happens in our brains concerns the activities of molecules and the interactions of electrons. Indeterminacy rules there, too: the next thought you have may well be partly determined by unpredictable molecular capering under the sway of Heisenberg's principle. There is no limit to the potential consequences.

The effect of Heisenberg's principle is further emphasized by another insight: chaos theory. We won't discuss the mathematics of chaos theory, but the guiding principle is that very slight differences in initial conditions can have enormous effects. Take an example: suppose a tiny puff of wind were to cause a butterfly's wing to flutter, distracting the attention of a tiger and causing him to miss a movement of the prey he was stalking. The prey saved from the tiger might later be killed and consumed by some starving hunter who lived to become, the next year, the father of a scientist who grew up to develop a cure for cancer. But absent the gentle puff and the insignificant butterfly, the cancer cure would have to wait for some other discoverer. Thousands of patients might die in the meantime.

Combined with the results of indeterminacy just discussed, chaos makes it clear that the detailed evolution of the universe is not predestined like a perfect bit of clockwork. It makes sense for us to will to be other than we are, and despite our limitations we can change things by our efforts. We do have a destiny but we are not helplessly trapped in a movie that merely plays itself out as filmed. The Holy Spirit makes suggestions but we are free to do as we decide. We are responsible. The universe has an infinite number of potential futures. This is our opportunity as well as our peril. This is how God created us: with the capacity to be our own beings and thus with the *other*ness necessary in objects of his love. The price we pay is the existence of incomprehensible evils such as crib death, holocausts, and inquisitions. The challenge is to be other than God without being estranged from him, as Siegfried was from Wotan.

Healing and Reunification

We don't want to be Siegfried to God's Wotan, and we don't have to be. Nothing I know of in science contradicts the belief that we can have a relationship with the ground of being. God creates us because he needs us. We have no way of knowing whether his love has other objects elsewhere in this universe[116] or in other universes or states of being. We do know what he demands of us: perfect love for him and for each other. Only one human being has ever met this demand. The rest of us fall far short. Of course we are still commanded to act as Jesus acted and taught; this is our response to all that we have been granted, the expression of our imperfect reflection of God's perfect love. It is our privilege and our joy to make this expression. But we cannot hope to reconcile ourselves to God, in good deeds or in any other way.

---

116 Astronomers are now estimating that there are probably billions of earth-sized planets in the universe. There is no apparent reason why life, and even humanity, may not have developed on many of these planets.

We are too important to God for him to let it go at that. I have mentioned the "New Being" several times. This term is a reference to St. Paul's triumphant declaration, quoted above in Chapter 7, "everything old has passed away; see, everything has become new!" Tillich put it this way:

A New Creation has occurred, a New Being has appeared; and we are all asked to participate in it...in the midst of the old creation there exists a New Creation, and that this New Creation is manifest in Jesus who is called the Christ." [117]

Christ is the savior – the healer – who reconciles us with God so that we can be accepted even though we are unacceptable. The meaning of being himself was clothed in flesh identical to that of an ordinary human being; he accepted torture and death to establish the New Being. He allows us to be saved, healed, reunited with God through the power of the meaning of being: love.

The Holy Spirit within us expresses God's continuing love, which is our continuing salvation. God's spirit is our breath. God accepts us; we accept God's acceptance to the extent that we allow ourselves to do so. Our acceptance does not enable us to lead lives of perfect love. Pogo was right to say, "We have met the enemy and he is us." We are estranged from the selves that God intends for us. To forgive ourselves – to be at one with ourselves – is to accept God's forgiveness, love, and acceptance, recognizing our unacceptability and embracing the miracle that we are nonetheless accepted.

Salvation is not escape from hellfire. Salvation is acceptance of the New Being starting right now, though it can be only a partial acceptance. Jesus reconciles us to God, to our neighbors, to ourselves. The New Being is not a life without problems. War, disease, hatred, and death will not disappear in the present epoch. But peace, healing, love, and new life are available to us. We have them in ever-greater abundance as we grow in our own acceptance of what is offered. And when our software is uploaded, we hope to have them unconditionally and eternally.

---

117 Tillich, Paul, *The New Being*, Lincoln, NE, University of Nebraska Press, 2005

CONCLUSION

There is no use looking to science for convincing evidence that there is a God or for convincing evidence that there is not. Science can prove neither the case for theism nor the case against it. The fundamental statements of religion are made on faith, or through revelation or mysticism or experience, not on the basis of proof. We can say that there is being – most of us think we see empirical evidence for that much – and conclude that there must be a ground of being, but even this conclusion is more a hunch than a rigorous deduction.

Yet in the final analysis the person who claims to reject all statements for which there is no clear evidence is deceiving himself. A peculiar but powerful theorem has established that there are statements in any mathematical system[118] that are true but cannot be proven; their truth or falsity cannot be determined with certainty. This theorem was itself proven in 1931 by Kurt Gödel, an Austrian-born mathematician. Similarly in life outside mathematics there are undoubtedly statements that are true but cannot be proven. No one can live without assuming the truth of certain unproved propositions. One has to decide which statements will be accepted without proof. The value of religion depends on the quality of life its followers experience, not on our ability to prove its precepts.

In real life there are no statements that can be known with the absolute certainty of a mathematical proof, but there are some that come pretty close. When religious beliefs contradict these statements it's time to reexamine them. For example, there is a great deal of evidence that the world is billions of years old. A dogmatic insistence that the true age is only a few thousand years may have some kind

---

118 Strictly speaking this theorem applies to any mathematical system sufficiently complex to include the integers: 1,2,3… and so on.

of truth: it may point, as the first chapter of Genesis does, to the merciful providence of God. But it cannot reasonably be considered a historical or scientific truth. When some theists insist that religion depends on statements that are clearly false, like the claim that the universe is young, they make it very hard for the rest of us to be theists.

There is no need for such stumbling blocks. In the preceding sections I have tried to point out how a well-accepted statement of the core beliefs of Christianity can be understood in a way that is consistent with what is known from other sources. This approach may need to restate some clauses in the Creed so that they look different, but the differences are superficial. The twenty-first century perspective, based on rational interpretation of empirical evidence available today, does no fundamental violence to the fourth, fifth, and sixth century perspective of the Nicene Creed. In fact what we know today illuminates what we learn from the early medieval clerics, who of course based their statements on the still earlier writers of scripture.

These perspectives are separated by one and a half millennia, but they correspond. I have tried to make their correspondence clear in what has gone before. For those who prefer a more explicit approach I have collected some of the twenty-first century understandings[119] under corresponding phrases from the Nicene Creed.

The result of this organization is contained in Appendix D.

---

119 By twenty-first century understanding I mean an understanding based on everything we know today. Virtually all of it was available before the beginning of this century and some of it far longer.

AFTERWORD: FAITH

I do not have faith that two plus two equals four. I know it for a fact. I cannot say the same about the statements in the Nicene Creed. I have tried to show that they are consistent with everything else we know, but that doesn't mean we know them to be facts like the facts of arithmetic.

Faith and knowledge are very different things. Children that I tutor in the Santa Fe public schools have been taught to do simple arithmetic by counting on their fingers. This is shocking to one who spent many hours being drilled in addition tables, but there is a tangible certainty to addition by finger-counting. While I was learning the tables I did get to see that six plus three added up to nine, but having learned that I stopped picturing it and relied on my confidence that I was remembering the answer correctly. The kids I tutor *know* how many fingers six plus three add up to because they see and count the fingers each time. No faith is required, at least until the sums exceed ten. Faith is the acceptance of things *not* seen. Doubt is an element of faith, and there is no doubt that two plus two equals four.

The subtle question arises, what does it mean to *know* something? Knowledge can be defined in a variety of ways. The simplest definition is to have no doubt, to be certain, but this definition has a problem: it applies even when the thing that is known is actually false. A confident student may *know*, like Huck Finn, that six times seven is thirty-five. But that doesn't make it true.

We'd like to eliminate the problem of *knowing* things that are false so we can extend the definition to require, in addition to our certainty, that the thing be true. I *know* that two plus two equals four. Not only am I certain of it but it is also true. Yet even this definition is not fully satisfactory. A horseplayer may be utterly certain that Equipoise will win the third race on Tuesday's card. And Equipoise may in fact win: somebody has to win. If that happens, the triumphant better will exclaim, "I *knew* it!" But in reality he didn't know; he was just lucky that time. If he really knew he would be a very rich horseplayer.

"Always certain, often wrong" is an unsatisfying definition of *know* and it keeps most dedicated horseplayers broke.

We really *know* something if we are certain of it, it is true, and there are solid grounds for our certainty: that is, our knowledge is based on evidence. I *know* that two and two make four because I can verify this fact by counting tangible objects, the way the kids I tutor count fingers.

The Meaning of Faith

Religious leaders have often demanded this kind of certainty regarding God. In one breath they assure us that God is infinite in every way and is beyond our comprehension. In the next they threaten that if we are not perfectly certain about specific human assertions of God's existence, nature, and benevolence, we're headed straight for Hell. Our certainty even has to extend to fine points of theology; if we get any of them wrong, or if we harbor the slightest doubt, we're fuel for the eternal furnace. It is not unknown for members of one Christian denomination to be told that members of another, equally respectable, denomination will be burned, not for any malfeasance but for their erroneous theology. A popular song of the 1950's asked, "How do I know? The Bible tells me so." The song's prescriptions were benign – faith, hope, charity, be good to your enemies – but some have used "the Bible tells me so" as a weapon to condemn anyone whose understanding of the scriptural message was discrepant.

That's not my understanding of faith. I have made a lot of statements about God in this essay. I don't *know* that a single one of them is true. They are not based on solid evidence. Rather than something we would today call a book the Bible is a collection of documents, some of them as brief as a single page. Each of these documents is called a book and represents the understanding of people who thought deeply about fundamental issues and reached the best conclusions they could in their times. The writers were inspired by the Holy Spirit to undertake these projects, but what they wrote was not a transcription of the literal voice of God. The fact that the Bible tells me something is a good reason for considering it thoughtfully but doesn't make each detail a divine revelation.

According to Karen Armstrong[120],

Today we tend to define "faith" as an intellectual assent to a creed, but, as we have seen, the biblical writers did not view faith in God as an abstract or philosophical belief. When they praise the "faith" of Abraham, they are not commending his orthodoxy (the acceptance of a correct theological opinion about God) but his trust, in rather the same way as when we say that we have faith in a person or an ideal. In the Bible, Abraham is a man of faith because he trusts that God would make good his promises, even though they seem absurd.

In those terms, faith today is a commitment to a body of thought about what lives we intend to lead in our own interests and in the interests of humankind. It's not a commitment that should be made lightly. It requires us to forswear actions that seem to offer us a superficial advantage – we shouldn't steal even if we are certain to get away with it – and to act always in our neighbor's best interest. I don't think we should undertake this commitment primarily in the hope of a reward in the afterlife, much as we might hope for an afterlife. The commitment is worth taking because it leads to the best life we know here and now.

The Nicene Creed, on its face, is a highly specific statement of "correct theological opinion". But it was actually a negotiated document: religious leaders got together and agreed on the details of what the church would teach. I imagine they all understood that God transcends feeble human attempts at understanding, but they decided to keep their stories straight. Final agreement – or near-agreement – took a couple of centuries. The theological details are not what matters. The *filioque* clause mentioned in the Preface, specifying that the Holy Spirit comes from the father *and the son*, has not the slightest effect on a person's ability to love and serve God and his neighbor. That's fortunate, because humans cannot possibly be certain whether this statement is true, false, or ultimately without meaning. (More

---

120 Armstrong, Karen, *A History of God*, New York, Ballantine Books, 1993

precisely, we cannot *know*. Unfortunately that doesn't stop some from being certain.)

A Framework

Coupled with scriptural revelation, the Creed as a whole is a framework on which to hang an understanding of our place and how to respond:

In the first paragraph we affirm that everything we have or will ever have is a gift of God.

In the second we affirm that he values us enough to make himself accessible: "God so loved the world that he gave his only begotten son..." The Creed jumps from Jesus's birth directly to his suffering and crucifixion, making no explicit mention of what came in between. Yet the core of the Creed – the strong nuclear force holding it together – is the manifestation, life, and teaching of Jesus, showing us how to live: "As I have loved you, so you must love one another."

In the third paragraph we affirm that the Holy Spirit makes it possible for us to seek a close relationship with God using the church, the prophetic tradition recorded in scripture, and the sacraments. There is also the promise of a continuing divine presence on earth and the hope of a life beyond the one here.

Faith in the sense described by Armstrong does not require that every tenet of the Nicene Creed or any other creed be accurate. Faith is a decision about the human response, about the way humans choose to live. The first paragraph expresses an awed, humble awareness of the vastness of the gift we have been given, the responsibility to care for it and to use it effectively, and the appropriateness of sharing what has been shared with us. This expression does not require a particular theological opinion; it is, or should be, universal. My philosophy professor once asked me how I knew there was a universe external to myself. I replied that if I had created the heavens and the earth I would be likely to remember doing so. The argument may not be rigorous but I still think I would remember such a task. Instead the universe is laid on for me. Spirituality begins with an appreciation of this fact.

The commandment to show active, creative, committed love in our dealings with everyone follows from the assertions of the second paragraph of the Creed. Even one who believed that Jesus of Nazareth never lived could respond to the central figure of the gospels, the embodiment of the meaning of being, and the teachings. The historical record is not essential and generally not helpful. The life commanded by Jesus is in any case the highest way we know of living, whether or not one accepts the Creed's assertions. We don't have to picture punishment for sinful behavior in this world or the next. Sinful behavior punishes itself: it closes us off from the loving relationships that give meaning to life. Hitler's punishment was not that he lost his war or that he died in a bunker. His punishment was self-inflicted: he condemned himself to live his life as Hitler.

The third paragraph of the Creed suggests a continuing spiritual consciousness transcending the daily struggle for food, clothing, and shelter, and giving deeper meaning to life. Humans do seek meaning in life. We are apparently built that way – some of the earliest esthetic artifacts ever found seem to express this seeking – and we don't need a particular theology to feel these yearnings. Faith is a commitment to pursue this deeper meaning, to live in ways congruent with our spiritual consciousness, even though we can never *know* the truth of our theological precepts.

Faith, then, is a response that does not require certain knowledge of what we are responding to. In the Gospel of John, Jesus says:[121]

"You know the way to the place where I am going."

Thomas said to him, "Lord, we do not know where you are going. How can we know the way?"

Jesus said to him, "I am the way…"

Jesus did not tell his disciples where he was going. He simply told them to follow "the way" – Jesus himself – to have faith that he knew the destination even if they didn't. Even those who doubt that Jesus ever lived two thousand years ago can experience him as alive today.

---

121 John 14:4-6

Christian faith includes a decision to open ourselves to the gift we have been given, to try to live the life of love, and to seek spiritual meaning in our lives. A liturgy somewhere refers to "the sure and certain hope of the resurrection." But "certain hope" is an oxymoron: we don't need to hope for something that is certain. The hope is sure, but it is no part of faith to be certain of the resurrection. Some people claim to be certain, but they don't *know*. Faith's response is a commitment to live in a particular way because this is the best way we know to live here and now. That's how we create our tentative Heaven – or our Hell, or, being human, elements of each – right now. This kind of life is its own reward, the greatest reward available to us. We surely hope for something more definitive in the next plane of existence, but if that is not to be we will never suffer disappointment.

BIBLIOGRAPHY

Adams, Douglas, *The Hitchhiker's Guide to the Galaxy*, Crown Publishers, Inc., New York NY, 1979

Armstrong, Karen, *A History of God*, New York, Ballantine Books, 1993

Barbour, Ian G., *When Science Meets Religion*, San Francisco, HarperCollins, 2000

Fagan, Brian, *Chaco Canyon: Archaeologists Explore the Lives of an Ancient Society*, New York NY, Oxford University Press, 2005

Greene, Brian, *The Elegant Universe*, New York and London, W. W. Norton & Company, 1999

Hawking, Steven W., *A Brief History of Time*, Toronto and New York, Bantam Books, 1988

Hawking, Steven and Mlodinow, Leonard, *A Briefer History of Time*, New York, Bantam Dell, 2005

The Holy Bible, New Revised Standard Version, New York, Oxford University Press, 1989

Johanson, Donald C. and Edey, Maitland A., *Lucy: The Beginnings of Humankind*, New York, Simon and Schuster, 1981

McLuhan, Marshall, *Understanding Media: The Extensions of Man*, New York, The McGraw-Hill Book Company, 1964

McPhee, John, *Annals of the Former World*, New York, Farrar, Straus and Giroux, 1998

Otto, Rudolph, *The Idea of the Holy*, Second Edition, Translated by John W. Harvey, London, Oxford, New York, Oxford University Press, 1950 (First Edition published 1923)

Silk, Joseph, *The Big Bang*, Third Edition, New York, W.H. Freeman and Company, 2001

Stone, Merlin, *When God Was a Woman*, New York, Harcourt Brace Jovanovich, 1978

Teilhard de Chardin, Pierre, *The Phenomenon of Man*, translated by Bernard Wall, New York, Harper & Row, originally published in French by Editions du Seuil, Paris, 1955

Tillich, Paul, *Systematic Theology*, Chicago, University of Chicago Press.
>   *Volume 1: Reason and Revelation. Being and God.* 1951.
>   *Volume 2: Existence and the Christ.* 1957.
>   *Volume 3: Life and the Spirit. History and the Kingdom of God.* 1963.

Tillich, Paul, *The New Being*, Lincoln, NE, University of Nebraska Press, 2005

Wright, Robert, *The Evolution of God*, New York, Little, Brown and Company, 2009

APPENDIX A: THE AGE OF ROCKS

"Christians desire that their children shall be taught all the sciences, but they do not want them to lose sight of the Rock of Ages while they study the age of rocks..."
William Jennings Bryan, speech prepared for the Scopes Trial

"I am more interested in the Rock of Ages than the age of rocks."
A character (based on Bryan) in "Inherit the Wind," Jerome Lawrence and Robert Edwin Lee's play based on the trial

We are interested in both and we find no incompatibility.

When James Hutton scandalized people by insisting that the earth was very old there were distinct limits on the kinds of statements he could make. As we saw in Chapter 2, a literal reading of the Bible – Bishop James Ussher made calculations based on the various ages reported for characters in the narrative – had led to the conclusion that the first events in Genesis occurred at a specified date in the year 4004 B.C.E. Hutton did not rely on scriptural accounts, but looked instead at the record in the rocks. Ussher's date was simply inconsistent with the evidence of Hutton's eyes. The angular unconformity at Jedburgh had obviously taken much longer than four thousand years to form, but Hutton could not say how much longer.

In the next century a great deal of effort was devoted to working out the timeline. Study of the rock record made it possible to show that one mass of rock had reached its present position more recently than another. In places – the Grand Canyon is a famous example – layers had been deposited one on top of the other, making the order clear. The part of this deposition we can now see is a layer cake. The rock of the lowest visible layers is over a billion years old; rock at the top is hundreds of millions of years old. Long after the rock layer cake had been formed the Colorado River sliced through it so we could get a look at the sequence. It's important to note that the sequence was quite incomplete, as many layers had been lost to erosion. The absence of a layer in the rock record does not imply that there is no gap in time; there can be gaps of many millions of years between layers now in contact. There's more missing than present but what is present presents a beautiful and fascinating story.

Additional evidence about the timeline came from the fossil record. If traces of a particular animal, in a specific phase of its evolution, are found in various places around the world, this is evidence that rock layers in those places have similar dates. Before numerical dates were possible, the efforts in stratigraphy (layers) and paleontology (fossils) led to a system of relative times associated with the rock record. The largest divisions, from oldest to youngest, are Precambrian, before there was an extensive fossil record; Paleozoic, when complex life forms covered the globe; Mesozoic, roughly the time of the dinosaurs; and Cenozoic, reaching to the present. Each of these largest divisions was subdivided several times leading eventually to a table of relative rock ages. Wherever rock of a certain type was found in a similar sequence of rock types, often in association with certain fossils, the inference was that the formation dated from, say, the Ludlovian stage of the Silurian period of the Paleozoic era.

This system of eras, stages, and periods is still in use, but initially it had one obvious drawback: it was a timetable with no times. Fossil and rock records could show that the dinosaurs of the Mesozoic came before the mammals of the Cenozoic, and certainly were far older than a few millennia, but there was no way to attach a number to the era. Until radiometric methods became available, determination of the ages of rocks was a qualitative, sequential matter. It was possible to infer which rocks were older but not to assign a numeric age. Dinosaurs have long been known to have been rampant during the Jurassic period of the Mesozoic era, but dating the beginning of that phenomenon to 208 million years ago only became possible more than a century after Hutton's death.

The Isotopic Egg Timer

What was needed was a very slow, very stable hourglass: an egg timer. To cook a three-minute egg, you place the egg in boiling water and turn the hourglass over. Sand runs from the upper chamber to the lower at a constant rate. The device is designed so that the upper chamber empties in three minutes; that's when you take the egg out of the water.

Nature provides something analogous through radioactivity but this hourglass measures much longer times, ranging from a few years to billions of years. And this hourglass is filled with isotopes, not sand. As described in Chapter 5, an atom comprises a nucleus surrounded by electrons. The number of protons – heavy charged particles – in the nucleus is equal to the number of electrons outside the nucleus. The electrons control the chemistry. They determine what the material is: iron, lead, oxygen... The nucleus also contains heavy but uncharged neutrons. The neutrons add to the weight of the nucleus but don't alter the chemical nature of the material because they don't affect the number of electrons. Different nuclei of the same material with different weights – that is, different numbers of neutrons – are called isotopes, and sophisticated equipment is needed to tell them apart. Some isotopes are stable, lasting a very long time. Others spontaneously disintegrate in much less than a second. An isotope is named on the basis of what material it is and on the weight of its nucleus. For example, carbon-14 is the isotope of carbon that has a nuclear weight of 14: the number of protons (6) and the number of neutrons (8) add up to 14. Carbon-12 is also carbon – it can't be separated chemically from carbon-14, as each has six electrons – but has a lighter nucleus containing 6 protons and 6 neutrons.

There is no predicting when a particular nucleus will disintegrate, but statistically the rate for a given isotope is very stable. The half-life is the time after which one half of the original number of nuclei have disappeared. It can be measured with great accuracy. For example, carbon-14 has a half-life of 5,730 years. That means that if you start with a million nuclei of carbon-14, you can be sure that 5,730 years later only half a million will remain. And 5,730 years after that half of the remaining half will remain. Turning this statement around, if you know how many carbon-14 atoms you started with and how many remain, you can calculate how long they have been decaying.

So carbon-14 can supply an egg timer appropriate for periods up to several times 5,730 years.

It's not easy to count the carbon-14 atoms that remain after a sample has been decaying for thousands of years, or to know how many there were to begin with, but there is a shortcut. During its lifetime an organism undergoes respiration. In this process it takes in known proportions of atmospheric carbon-12, which is stable and does not decay, and of carbon-14, which does decay. When the organism dies, respiration ceases and no more carbon is taken in. That's the point when the egg timer starts. The amount of carbon-12 remains constant but the carbon-14 decays, so the amount remaining keeps decreasing. The ratio of carbon-14 to carbon-12 becomes gradually less, at a steady rate that has been measured accurately in the laboratory and tabulated in reference books. You can't measure this ratio by chemical techniques, but with modern physical techniques it can be measured. With the carbon-14/carbon-12 ratio and a known value for the rate at which it declines with time, an accurate clock is formed, telling how long ago the organism died. Paleontological specimens can be dated at ages up to about 60,000 years by this method.

Turning the Egg Timer Over

The carbon-14/carbon-12 system is just one of many radiometric systems that are used for various dating jobs. Others start the clock in different ways. One of the most valuable systems is based on lead and two different isotopes of uranium. Uranium-235 decays to lead-207, and uranium-238 decays to lead-206; this system provides two different clocks. As described in Chapter 4, heavy elements like lead and uranium were created in stars and spewed into the universe at large, forming part of the substance of our planet. Certain crystals called zircons incorporate significant amounts of uranium – both isotopes – into their structure. But zircons do not incorporate lead. The only lead in a zircon is produced there by decay of uranium. Thus when the egg timer was turned over millions of years ago, the ratio of lead to uranium was zero: there was no lead. The lead/uranium ratio increased at a steady known rate until, in modern times, the ratio is measured and the interval since the egg timer was turned over is easily calculated. Note that this time we measure the amount of the decay product that has built up in the sample rather than the amount of the original product that has disappeared, as in the carbon-14/carbon-12 system.

What does it mean to "turn the egg timer over?" Zircons form at high temperatures. Under these conditions, any lead that is formed diffuses out of the zircon. In effect, the clock always reads zero: no lead. When the zircon has cooled to a low enough temperature, the lead can no longer get out of the zircon. It begins to accumulate, and the clock starts to run. The egg timer has been turned over. This system, like most radiometric dating systems (carbon-14/carbon-12 is an exception), measures the time since the zircon cooled to a temperature at which the resulting product, in this case lead, could no longer escape.

There are many other radiometric dating systems, measuring different materials, different rock systems, and different starting points. They depend on isotopes with differing half-lives, and therefore are sensitive to different durations: uranium-238/thorium-230 is best for ages of several hundred thousand years, while samarium-147/neodymium-143 and potassium-40/argon-40 can measure ages in the billions of years.

The qualitative approach was still useful after radiometric techniques made it possible to assign dates. Index fossils permitted dates measured in one locality to be carried over to other places where similar fossils were found. For example,[122] pigs found along the Omo River, in Ethiopia, evolved over a period of four million years. It happens that there had been frequent eruptions in the area, and the volcanic tuff they distributed was widespread. Tuff can be accurately dated radiometrically. Pig fossils could in turn be dated on the basis of their placement relative to the tuff. The tuff dated the layer, the

122 Johanson, Donald C. and Edey, Maitland A., Lucy: The Beginnings of Humankind, New York, Simon and Schuster, 1981

layer dated the pig fossils found in it. Then the pig sequences could be used as a standard for other areas where similar pig fossils were found and where there were no good samples for radiometric dating. Comparison of a new fossil with dated specimens from Omo allowed the age of the new fossil, and of the rock it was found in, to be determined quite reliably.

Radiometric techniques, and methods for propagating their dates more widely, turned the qualitative system of eras, stages, and periods into a quantitative timeline, assigning ages to rocks that in some cases formed when Earth first solidified. The oldest rocks found on our planet come from four billion years ago.

APPENDIX B:
SOFTWARE IN THE CHROMOSOME

I said in Chapter 6 that the software is not the sweater. That's also true in the case of chromosomes, but like a knitting pattern the software tells a great deal about the molecule itself. Each chromosome is a molecule of deoxyribonucleic acid (DNA). DNA is enormous by molecular standards, containing billions of atoms. A DNA molecule comprises two strands that wind around each other to form the famous double helix sketched in Figure 3a.

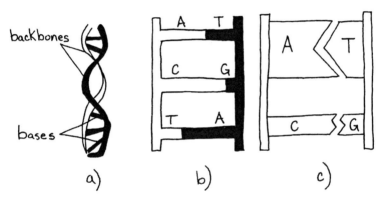

Figure 3. (a) The double helix formed by two backbones twisted around each other, with bases protruding from the backbones. (b) Bridges A-T or C-G form stable connections of constant length between the two strands. (c) The binding of complementary bases.

Each strand has a backbone with millions of little blocks sticking out from it. Each of these blocks is a base, an entity familiar to chemists in other settings. Each base reaches from its backbone toward a corresponding base on the other strand's backbone so that the bases meet near the midpoint and form a bridge between the strands, as shown in Figure 3b. Of the many bases chemists know, DNA uses only four: adenine, cytosine, guanine, and thymine, abbreviated A, C, G, and T, respectively. The bases attached to one strand's backbone can come in any order. The pattern of bases forms a program, or code, like the pattern that formed the simple program discussed in the main text. But in the case of DNA there are four program elements, A, C, G, and T, instead of the two elements, 0 and 1, common in computer work.

A strand of DNA is defined by a long program, a sequence made up of these four elements. To make up a random example, it might be ACAGTCGGAAT... and so on for tens of thousands of pages: the molecular program is a hundred million letters long. A short group of consecutive bases within the long strand constitutes a gene. A gene acts as an action instruction to the cell: it tells the cell to manufacture a particular protein. This is the mechanism by which the genes control the activities and development of the cell.

Complementary Bases, Complementary Strands

The key to the cell's ability to reproduce a strand of DNA lies in the sizes and shapes of the bases. Adenine and thymine fit together to form a bridge between two strands, and guanine and cytosine fit together and form a bridge of the same length, as shown in Figure 3c. So if the bridge is formed of the combination A-T or the combination C-G, it is of a standard length; the standard-length bridges keep the two strands separated by a constant distance. The bases adenine and thymine are thus complementary, as are the bases cytosine and guanine.

If one strand of the complete DNA molecule is present, a second, complementary, strand can be formed one base at a time. The process, carried out under the catalyzing influence of a series of chemical triggers called enzymes, is quite complex, but the resulting coding is straightforward. The second strand is complementary, base by base, to the first. Our example of a segment of one strand was the sequence ACAGTCGGAAT. The first base of this strand is A (adenine), so the first base of the second strand would be T (thymine) because that is the complement to A (adenine). Similarly, the second base of the new strand would be G (guanine), the complement to the second base of the original strand, C (cytosine). Continuing the process, we see that the new segment would be TGTCAGCCTTA.

The base at each point of the new strand is the one complementary to the base at the corresponding point of the old strand. The new strand will not incorporate a base other than the complementary one at a given point.

When the process is complete a second strand has been formed, with each base on the second strand complementary to the corresponding base on the first. The new strand and the old twist around each other; the pair of strands forms the double helix that is a complete DNA molecule. The entire second strand is described as complementary to the first. Then if the two strands are unwound from each other, as occurs naturally under the control of enzymes, each strand can provide the pattern for another strand. The second strand will be the pattern for a strand complementary to itself, and thus identical to the first strand. The first strand will similarly be the basis for a strand identical to the second. The outcome is that one double-stranded DNA molecule has reproduced, or doubled, itself.

The process can be repeated over and over, and the amount of material produced is remarkable. If this doubling occurred twenty times, over a million copies of the molecule would be formed. Forty doublings would produce many trillions of molecules. Once nature had learned to produce DNA, enormous amounts of identical genetic material could be produced very quickly.

APPENDIX C:
DINOSAURS AND THE *DEUS EX MACHINA*

In ancient Greek theater, sometimes the playwright would get his characters into a predicament whose solution was beyond the capability of human beings. As the denouement approached the audience would hear the noise of machinery: sometimes a crane, sometimes a device for lifting a man through a trapdoor in the stage. A god would be seen, lowered or raised onto the stage. With his powers, the *deus ex machina* – the god from the machine – would impose a solution and everybody could go home satisfied. This kind of writing was criticized even then on the basis, as we might express it in modern times, that the resolution should arise organically from the plot. But playwrights have continued to use the device to this day. And occasionally the effect pops up in real life.

We have claimed that God created humans as objects for his love. We are descended from primates, which are mammals, not from reptilian dinosaurs. But from 250 B.C.E. until 65 B.C.E. dinosaurs dominated life on Earth. Mammals did exist but they were small and inoffensive. They didn't challenge the dinosaurs; they hid from them. For 185 million years the big lizards sat at the top of the heap, and there was nothing in sight that could unseat them. It looked as if God would have to have love objects with reptilian brains.

Then, somehow, the dinosaurs all died. The fossil record is clear: One instant dinosaurs ruled; the next instant (within the experimental limits of dating fossils) they were gone. It took only months or a few years; there is even a hypothesis under which it happened in a matter of hours. More than half of the animals on the planet died with the dinosaurs in a great mass extinction. This point in time is called the C-T boundary because it's the boundary between the cretaceous era – the dinosaurs' time – and the succeeding tertiary epoch with proliferation of mammals and birds.[123] The event is

---

123 There is considerable evidence, as remarked in Chapter 11, that modern birds are descended from dinosaurs.

called the cretaceous extinction. The fact that the dinosaurs had been extinguished in a very short time was well known. The reason for this event – what a dinosaur historian, if they'd had any, would surely call a disaster of biblical proportions – was a mystery.

The Iridium-Rich Layer

In the late 1970's Luis and Walter Alvarez studied a thin layer of clay – it was just one centimeter thick – dating from the C-T boundary period 65 million years ago. They found that this layer had thirty times as much iridium as it should have had. The element iridium is rare on Earth. The thin layer has since been found in many places all over the planet, always containing too much iridium and always with 65 million year-old rocks. It was known that some asteroids have high concentrations of iridium. On the basis of these clues the Alvarezes suggested that the iridium in the C-T layer came from a huge iridium-rich asteroid that crashed into our planet. The impact would have caused an explosion and left iridium debris on the surface everywhere. The amount of iridium deposited suggested a projectile six miles in diameter. (For comparison, Mount Everest is almost six miles high.) Such an object crashing into our planet would have devastating consequences: a huge explosion, fires over much of the globe, and acid rain resulting from the carbon dioxide released by the fires. Very large amounts of iridium would have blown as dust through the skies, eventually to settle back to earth to form the iridium-rich layer. While airborne, the dust would fill the skies and block most sunlight, causing a dark cold period that large plant and animal species might find unsurvivable. Strong support for the Alvarez theory came in 1990 when Alan Hildebrand found evidence in the Yucatan of a possible impact site. The crater was radiometrically dated at 65 million years old. Its size was consistent with the impact crater from an object six miles in diameter.

The details of the Cretaceous extinction are still being worked out. It has also been postulated that massive volcanic activity could have contributed to the extinction. And a far larger impact crater, dated to about the same time, has recently been discovered in India.

What is nevertheless clear is this: sixty-five million years ago mammals had no way to overcome the might of the enormous dinosaurs. The development of the large carnivorous mammals we are descended from didn't seem possible. Then Earth experienced a *deus ex machina* in the form of one or more giant punches in the belly: the impacts. The small mammals, while they couldn't compete with dinosaurs, could somehow dig in and ride out the effects of the impact that killed the larger creatures. The bombardment solved the mammals' dinosaur problem and allowed them to supplant their saurian competitors.

That's how humans evolved looking like us rather than like monsters from Jurassic Park.

APPENDIX D:
A MODERN LOOK AT THE NICENE CREED

My goal in the preceding chapters has been to show how the contemporary scientific understanding and the traditional religious understanding are in harmony. In order to make this harmony explicit, the following paragraphs present my understanding, based on what I know of science and of religion, with the corresponding clauses of the Nicene Creed.

The Father
We believe in one God,

God is the eternal ground who is the basis of being itself. Without God, the ground of being, there would not be anything: not a thing would be. (I'm trying to avoid saying, "There would be nothing," which seems to make "nothing" into something that would be.) Being is all or none: either there is being or there is not. There is only one ground in which all that is has its being. That is to say there is one God: no more, no less.

…the Father,

The symbol of God as father celebrates the fact that he gives us our existence and guides us with parental love and authority. Jesus pointed to the love of a human parent as a reflection, however dim, of God's fatherly love. In the Lord's Prayer he addressed God as "our Father."

…the Almighty,

It is traditional to speak of God as omnipotent, omniscient, and omnipresent. His omnipresence follows from his identity as the ground of being: wherever being is the ground is present. God is obviously very powerful and very informed but we don't actually have any way of knowing whether he is *omni*potent and *omni*scient. There are famous cavils about omnipotence such as, "Could God tie a knot that he couldn't untie?" We have stated in Chapter 6 that even

God could not draw a circle for which the value of π was changed. But rather than real limitations on his power these refer to logical inconsistencies or logical necessities. We have also stated, in Chapter 12, that even God does not know the velocity of an electron once its position is exactly determined, or the exact moment when a nucleus will emit an α particle. These are not limitations on God's knowledge either, but a recognition that science tells us the electron and the α particle do not *have* fixed futures. If there were real limits to God's power or knowledge we wouldn't know about them. They would be at a level far above our understanding. He has no limits we can be aware of. For our purposes God is omnipotent and omniscient – almighty and all-knowing – and we celebrate the fact that he is always with us.

...maker of heaven and earth, of all that is, seen and unseen.

God is the creator of our universe and of all that exists, here or elsewhere. A Eucharistic prayer in the Episcopal church states that he prepared for the universe before the beginning of time. That's equivalent to saying, in the language of Chapter 3, that at t_0 he had already set the initial conditions. God's creativity is not limited to what is present here on Earth or even to what exists in our universe. God is eternal: there was being already at t_0.

The Son

We believe in one Lord, Jesus Christ, the only Son of God, eternally begotten of the Father,

The meaning of being, also called the Word or the logos, is eternally with the ground of being. Meaning depends on being in a logical sense, though meaning was always present with being. The Word, who is the ground of meaning, was miraculously clothed in flesh and entered history at a very recent instant of time. But while we live virtually as contemporaries of Jesus, the Word is eternal as the ground of being is eternal: being and its meaning are coeternal. As being has only one meaning, so there is only one Word, one Christ, one Son.

…God from God, Light from Light, true God from true God, begotten, not made, of one Being with the Father. Through him all things were made.

The Word is God – being and its meaning are inseparable – and is the Light of the world. Meaning gives light to the world. The meaning of being is made manifest – is illuminated – by its incarnation in Jesus. All that has being in the ground of being has meaning in the ground of meaning. St. Paul calls God's son "…the image of the invisible God".[124]

For us and for our salvation he came down from heaven:

The estrangement of humans from God, symbolized by the mythic story of the fall of Adam,[125] is a condition that humankind cannot rectify on its own. It is out of his love for humankind, the drive to conquer estrangement, that God sent his son to manifest the meaning of being.

…by the power of the Holy Spirit he became incarnate from the Virgin Mary, and was made man.

The man Jesus of Nazareth was born naturally to two ordinary humans. We know his mother as Mary and presume his father to have been Joseph, though his father's identity, while interesting, is not fundamentally important. Jesus was in every way human, conceived with DNA from both of his human parents, reared normally for his time, though showing precocious understanding in discussions with teachers in the temple in Jerusalem.[126] And yet he was the Christ: the anointed one. In a true miracle with no trace of an explanation in terms of physical laws, this true man gave a body to the Word itself, the meaning of being. Though his birth as a man was ordinary, he was anointed as a unique being. He was born to a virgin in the sense that neither his mother not anyone else had any prior experience of such a phenomenon. Saint Paul describes the whole of creation as groaning in labor pains in anticipation of the coming of the Light.

---

124 Colossians 1:15

125 The word *humankind* in Genesis 1:27 is a rendering of the Hebrew *Adam*.

126 Luke 2:46-47

For our sake he was crucified under Pontius Pilate; he suffered death and was buried.

In his life and teaching Jesus revealed in greater detail the meaning that was manifested by his being. The meaning is love. As God created us to be the objects of his love, he commanded us through the Christ to love God and to love our fellows. By teaching and example Jesus redefined love of neighbor, not as a passive emotion felt toward a limited community of those near and dear, but as an active, all-encompassing, creative, committed passion to care for our fellow humans and to help them to reach their full potential. The narrative of his life, including such parables as the Good Samaritan, makes clear that we are to love *all* our neighbors, *all* the time. His life defined what he meant when he said, "*As I have loved you*, so you must love…" Jesus showed the depth of his love and the strength of his commitment in his life and death. Having lived the life of love, Jesus accepted torture and death; God withheld nothing from us, not even his beloved son. The agony of Jesus was real, and he did not accept it easily. He screamed in pain, he cried out for deliverance, but he was never estranged from the Father. His death was a real death followed by a real entombment.

On the third day he rose again in accordance with the Scriptures;

About forty hours after he breathed his last, the disciples began to learn that their experience of Jesus had not ended with his crucifixion. The women who went to the tomb to anoint his body came to the realization that he was to be sought among the living, not the dead. He had risen. It was as if a rock of ignorance had been rolled away, allowing the women to enter the tomb and discover the central fact of human existence. Jesus had inhabited his followers. He was with them, as he is with us, eternally.

…he ascended into heaven and is seated at the right hand of the Father.

Heaven is not a place in the sense that Santa Fe, New Mexico is a place. The ascension of Jesus is a transformation in state of being, leaving behind the body that had served its purpose. Jesus ceased to be limited by a location in space and time and became accessible to humankind in all times and places. His seat "at the right hand of the Father" is not a physical position but a relationship with the ground of being. It recalls the position of the most trusted advisor sitting at the right hand of a monarch, sharing in power, authority, and governance. The disciples quarreled over positions of honor, seeking places next to Jesus in the coming era. But Jesus rebuked them: it was not his calling, or theirs, to seek honor.

He will come again in glory to judge the living and the dead, and his kingdom will have no end.

When Jesus walked the earth, his physical presence was necessary to communication. People did not ask questions or make requests of Jesus when he was out of earshot. But, having ascended into Heaven, he is with all of us in a new way. Leaving us, he became more present than ever. He has come again. His second coming is not an apocalyptic event, but a continuing presence that is more fully realized as humankind gradually becomes more attuned to it. His judgment is merciful and his presence signals the New Being, which begins for each of us here on Earth and continues through eternity.

The Holy Spirit

We believe in the Holy Spirit, the Lord, the giver of life, who proceeds from the Father and the Son.

The Holy Spirit, the breath of being, whispers to humans throughout history, inspiring them to understand. The Spirit gives life. The ground of being and the meaning of being are the source of the breath of being. The Spirit is the ground of revelation, the basis of our day-to-day experience of God. Since it is this experience that gives our lives meaning, the Spirit animates the chemical clay of our bodies. In this sense, the Spirit is the soul of being.

With the Father and the Son he is worshipped and glorified.

The Spirit is recognized as a Person integral to the Trinity, revealing to humankind the creative and redemptive acts of the Father and Son. The Spirit is God, as the Father is God and the Son is God.

He has spoken through the Prophets.

God is a principle of creative love whose love leads to his creativity. Since love is the desire for closer union with another, to be complete God needs an *other* to be love's object. To be other than God, and thus to be the objects of his love, humans must have freedom. It follows that God's communication must not be overpowering.

God has revealed himself throughout human history, but for a revelation to be complete, humankind must be prepared to receive it. Scripture evolved as understanding developed. The early scriptural moral understanding was the highest humankind was prepared to receive when it was written down. Later, moral understanding was far more completely expressed in the life and teaching of Jesus, where love for God and fellow subsumes the detailed instructions of earlier times. Morality in the New Being is based on Christ's commandment to love and on the understanding of this commandment provided by his life and teaching. The teaching of Jesus is always positive, exhorting us to find ways to help all of our neighbors to achieve a fulfilling relationship with God and each other.

We believe in one holy catholic and apostolic Church.

The church is the fellowship of God's people, deriving its holiness from its devotion to God. As there is one God there is one fellowship, open to all. The church is thus catholic: that is, universal. Its task is to carry on the work of the apostles. The teachings of scripture, and in particular of Jesus and his apostles, are the basis of the church's understanding.

Any visible church is a human approximation of the one church. The scores of Christian sects invariably are human institutions and manifest human shortcomings. They do great good, and sometimes sponsor great harm. Disagreements are to be expected from imperfect human institutions. Yet as representations of the one church, the visible churches are the primary institutions through which his followers do God's work in the world.

We acknowledge one baptism for the forgiveness of sins.

Our evolving understanding is supported by the Holy Spirit's communication to us through prayer and sacraments. Prayer is a conversation in which we get in touch with God. The principal sacraments are baptism and Eucharist. In Eucharist our senses perceive the odor and taste of the wine, the sound of the breaking bread and its tactile sensation on our tongues, and we perceive in a new way the living presence of Christ. Baptism is the entry into the church: the fellowship of believers, the communion of saints, where our state of sin, of estrangement from God, is healed.

We look for the resurrection of the dead, and the life of the world to come.

Even with the example of Jesus, no human since his time has achieved the perfect, unceasing, creative, committed, all-encompassing love to which we are called. It is Jesus who allows us to be at one with God. The Holy Spirit breathes to us that the least of us is accepted despite the unacceptability of the best of us. Our estrangement is cured only by the grace of God. Our acceptance of this grace allows us to enter the New Being. Salvation is actual to the extent that we accept what is offered, and becomes unconditional when our software is uploaded.

INDEX

D

E

F

ABOUT THE AUTHOR

W. Scott Andrus was born in new York City and brought up in the (then) semi-bucolic borough of Queens. Early in life he sampled Protestant churches, being dedicated as a Baptist infant, baptized as a Presbyterian baby, and confirmed as a Lutheran teenager. He is now a member of an Episcopal congregation.

Indulging a youthful interest in science, Scott went on to receive his Ph.D. in Physics from Stony Brook University in 1967, using a nuclear reactor at Brookhaven National laboratory for his research. His research interests have ranged widely, including neutron scattering from liquids, X-ray astronomy, tissue culture, and surface analysis. He spent over two decades developing better ways to treat serious diseases, working in the areas of cardiology, urology, otology, X-ray interpretation, endoscopy, lasers, fiber optics, and radioactive source placement. He is responsible for several patents and dozens of publications in these fields.

Scott married Marge in 1974 and is delighted that she has continued to put up with him. They have lived in Boston, California, and Minnesota; in retirement they have settled in Santa Fe. Scott's current interests include acting, writing, singing in the choir, training Toby the agnostic Golden Retriever, hiking, skiing, and golf.

Being, Meaning, and Breath was written over a period of nine years, mostly in Santa Fe but with sporadic vacation efforts in Tuscany, Venice, Paris, Spain, and various ski areas. The nine writing years summarize the results of more than half a century pondering the concerns he writes about, beginning in childhood in New York. It was brought to a head when Scott heard a radio pundit claiming that science had eliminated the possibility of religion. This book answers with a firm "No way!"

If you want to continue the discussion, either to set him straight or to agree with him and add further light, you are invited to join him in the Forum on his website, Beingmeaningandbreath.com.

CPSIA information can be obtained at www.ICGtesting.com
Printed in the USA
LVOW071643100312

272514LV00001B/27/P